Telegram forms
and tokens

Portable
typewriter, 1969

1980s pager

1990s mobile
phone

Wearable
computer,
produced
in 1998

Telephone
operator's
gas mask

The Diamond Sutra,
a Buddhist scroll
printed in A.D. 868

1909 Report on "telegraphist's cramp,"
now known as repetitive strain injury

1880s Morse code
transmitter

EYEWITNESS BOOKS

MEDIA &
COMMUNICATIONS

Written by
CLIVE GIFFORD

Ground-to-air
signal

Ground-to-air
signal indicating
direction

Early radio and
receiver

Stone marker, or
cairn, indicating
direction

Stone marker,
or cairn,
indicating a
left turn

ALFRED A. KNOPF • NEW YORK

A DORLING KINDERSLEY BOOK

Project editor Carey Scott
Art editor Joanne Connor
Senior managing editor Linda Martin
Senior managing art editor Julia Harris
Production Kate Oliver
Picture researcher Frances Vargo
DTP designer Andrew O'Brien
Jacket designer Chris Branfield
Special photography Steve Gorton

This is a Borzoi Book published by Alfred A. Knopf, Inc.

This Eyewitness® Book has been conceived by
Dorling Kindersley Limited and Editions Gallimard.

First American edition, 1999

www.randomhouse.com/kids

Printed in Singapore
0 9 8 7 6 5 4 3 2 1

Library of Congress Cataloging-in-Publication Data
Gifford, Clive.
Media and communications / Clive Gifford – 1st American edition.
p.   cm. — (Eyewitness books; v. 74)
Includes index.

ISBN 0-375-80223-1 (trade)
ISBN 0-375-90223-6 (lib. bdg)

1. Communication — History.
2. Mass media — History.
I. Title. II. Title: Media and communications
P90 .G474 1999
302.2 — dc21

99-22723

Color reproduction by
Colourscan, Singapore
Printed in China
by Toppan Printing Co., (Shenzhen) Ltd.

Ink blotter from
a telegraph office

Feather quill

Sanitary telephone
mouthpiece

International
phone cards

Space age television, 1969

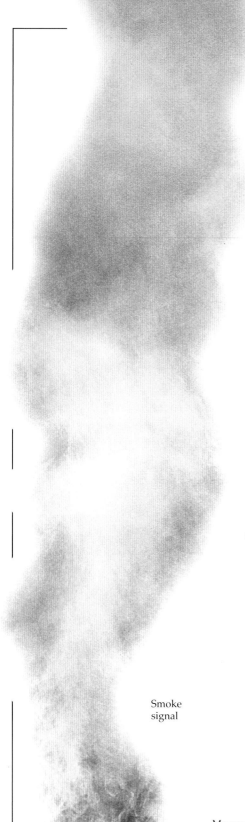

Smoke
signal

Morse code
transmitter

Powerbook
computer,
1998

Contents

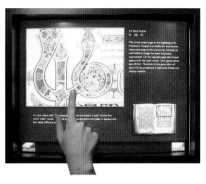

Detail of
a digital
gospel

Turning the
pages of a
digital gospel

What are media?

COMMUNICATION — the sharing of information, ideas, and thoughts — is a vital part of life for all of us. The different methods that allow us to communicate are called media. A postcard to a friend, a telephone call, and a computer disk holding homework are all types of media. When media are used to communicate to thousands of people at the same time — television, newspapers, and advertising billboards — they are known as mass media. Some of these have developed beyond simple methods of communication to become sophisticated tools, capable of persuading and influencing large numbers of people.

NOTING IT DOWN
Writing was developed so that language could be recorded permanently. On this Sumerian clay tablet, over 5,000 years old, is some of the earliest known writing. It records a tally of the number of sheep and goats in a part of Mesopotamia (Iraq), using a writing system called cuneiform.

Cuneiform signs were made with a wedge-shaped stylus

Two men usually worked together at the press

Rosie the Riveter, the symbol of a successful propaganda campaign during World War II

A GREAT LEAP FORWARD
One of the greatest advances in communication was the adoption of movable-type printing presses in 15th-century Europe. For the first time, multiple copies of documents could be produced quickly and cheaply. Ideas and information were circulated to large numbers of people through the mass production of books, pamphlets, and newssheets. The printing press was the first instrument of mass communication.

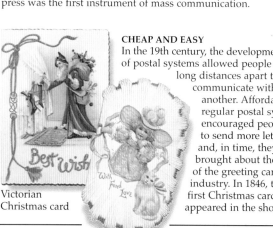

CHEAP AND EASY
In the 19th century, the development of postal systems allowed people long distances apart to communicate with one another. Affordable, regular postal systems encouraged people to send more letters and, in time, they also brought about the start of the greeting card industry. In 1846, the first Christmas cards appeared in the shops.

Victorian Christmas card

Best Wish

With Fond Love

Telephone produced for American Telephone and Telegraph company

Metal telephone, produced in 1937

HOUSEHOLD PHONE
Telecommunications are media that allow information to be transmitted over long distances by electrical signals. The telephone is the most successful of these media. Invented in 1876, it is still one of the most widely used forms of communication, because it provides instant, private contact between two or more people. Many people now have mobile phones.

MOVING PICTURES
The arrival of moving pictures created two powerful new media — movies and television. Films produced by big Hollywood studios, such as 20th Century Fox, attracted huge audiences from the 1920s onward. After World War II, the television age began in earnest, with millions tuning in for their nightly entertainment.

MARKETING WITH MEDIA
Some products, such as cola drinks, are known to millions of people. This is a result of many decades of advertising their names and logos in every available medium throughout the world. Clever marketing ensures the product always has a high profile in every country in which it is sold.

PROPAGANDA POWER
During World War II, jobs in traditionally male industries, such as shipbuilding, became vacant as men enlisted in the armed forces. In the United States and Britain, a vigorous campaign was launched to persuade women into these industries. Posters featuring an image of a strong female worker, called Rosie the Riveter, urged women to "do the job he left behind." The campaign was so successful that, when the war ended, it was difficult to persuade women back into their homes.

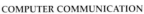

Typing at a computer keyboard has replaced handwriting for much written communication

COMPUTER COMMUNICATION
Computers have already made great changes in the ways we communicate. They are used to speed up or improve established forms of communication, such as telephone systems. And they have generated brand-new methods of communication, such as the Internet and virtual reality, which will be with us long into the 21st century.

This device, called a mouse, is used to control some of the computer's functions

Early communication

Cave painting of bison

THE FIRST PAINTINGS
Cave paintings over 20,000 years old have been found in Europe, Australia, and South America. They often depict animals, probably species that were commonly hunted. Early people were also fascinated by their own form, and paintings of human hands have been located as far apart as France and Argentina.

CONCH SHELL
Our ancestors found that blowing into certain shells, such as the giant conch, produced a loud, distinctive sound. This sound was ideal for communicating a simple warning or greeting. Conch shells were used by Inca messengers in parts of South America and by many societies in Asia and the Pacific.

PEOPLE HAVE COMMUNICATED with each other since prehistoric times. Animals and birds communicate through movement, cries, and grunts — our primitive ancestors did the same. Gradually, early people started to learn how to use natural items, such as shells, and how to make simple tools, to aid communication. They lit fires to send important messages, and they used naturally occurring pigments, such as clay and chalk, to produce the first paintings. Experts believe that early communication was used primarily to establish a person's or a group's identity with another group, and to convey warnings, greetings, and news of victories in battles.

Cave painting of hands

Sound is amplified by the chamber

A single column of smoke means "The camp is here."

SMOKE SIGNALS
For centuries, smoke signals were used as a form of communication. Damp grass or leaves were placed on a strong-burning fire, creating a large column of smoke that could be seen from a great distance.

Cords are pressed to produce tonal sounds that resemble language

West African talking drum

COMMUNICATING WITH MUSIC
In many African countries, drums were used for thousands of years as a method of communication. They conveyed simple messages or honored a great chief. In some West African societies, complicated drum stories, played on special talking drums, even related the tribe's history.

Three columns of
smoke indicate
that "There is
good news."

*Damp leaves
or grass will
encourage
thick smoke*

NATIVE AMERICAN SIGNALS
Contrary to popular belief,
the Native Americans did
not spell out complicated
messages with dozens of
puffs of smoke. In reality,
simple smoke signals
were used to communicate
particular messages. A
single column of smoke
may have been used by
the leaders of nomadic
tribes to show where a
new camp was; three
columns of smoke could
indicate good news, such
as victory in battle.

Spreading the word

WORDS AND LANGUAGE developed out of people's need to communicate with each other about the world around them and their relationships. Much early language is believed to have been concerned with survival, pointing out where danger lay and how to avoid it. Communication, in the form of greetings, conversation, and entertainment, can give people great pleasure, but words can also inform (or misinform), instruct, and persuade. The ability to discuss and debate topics in a clear, articulate way is useful to everyone. For centuries politicians, philosophers, and religious leaders have all used persuasive speaking to get their messages across more forcefully. Today, mass broadcast media can relay words around the world instantly, making clever and considered speech more important than ever.

SOCRATES
The ancient Greeks had a very strong tradition of oral communication. The famous philosopher Socrates (469–399 B.C.) did not leave any writings. He preferred to learn and pass on knowledge by rigorous questioning and examination of others' answers. This process is still known today as Socratic dialogue.

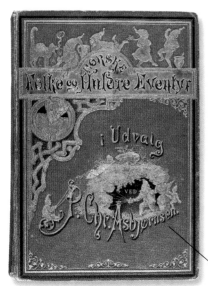

This collection is called Folk and Witch Tales

FOLK STORIES
Throughout history, stories and fairy tales have been passed from parents to children orally. Over generations of retelling, different versions of the same stories can appear. In many cases, nobody knows who the first storyteller was. Eventually, some of these stories were written down in books, such as this collection of Norwegian folktales.

RING-AROUND-A-ROSY
Many people think of children's nursery rhymes as meaningless entertainment, but some have very serious origins. Ring-around-a-rosy is believed to be about the bubonic plague that struck Europe in the medieval era. *"All fall down"* describes the grisly death resulting from the plague.

WORD TRAVELS FAST
Stories, songs, and rhymes can travel the world without the help of modern mass media like radio or television. These children in Puerto Rico are playing a game based on an old English rhyme called "London Bridge Is Falling Down" — even though London Bridge is over 4,349 miles (7,000 km) from Puerto Rico.

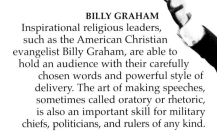

BILLY GRAHAM
Inspirational religious leaders, such as the American Christian evangelist Billy Graham, are able to hold an audience with their carefully chosen words and powerful style of delivery. The art of making speeches, sometimes called oratory or rhetoric, is also an important skill for military chiefs, politicians, and rulers of any kind.

The religious leader Billy Graham giving a speech

HEALTHY COMMUNICATING
Oral communication is a very effective method of getting across important information. Above, a health educator in Burkina Faso, Africa, teaches women about the importance of proper health care during pregnancy. Community workers are helping to reduce infant mortality (death) and increase general health in many parts of the world.

Men smoke as they listen to the story

In Arab societies, shoes are usually removed before sitting

PROFESSIONAL STORYTELLING
The Arab societies of the Middle East were famous for their tradition of professional storytelling. For centuries, these storytellers, known as *rawis*, performed for money in market squares and coffeehouses. Crowds would gather to hear their expertly told tales of adventure and romance. Many of these tales were collected and published in the book of stories known as the *Arabian Nights* or the *Thousand and One Nights*.

Body language and gestures

WE MAY THINK OF WORDS as being the most important way that people communicate, but body language, which is often unconscious, also plays a significant part. Facial expression, gestures, and physical posture all send out particular messages. Some professional people, such as interviewers, police, and psychiatrists, are specially trained to interpret body language. Yet, even though we may not be aware of it, we are all capable of receiving messages communicated to us by body language.

Action is played out on stage

Direct eye contact is maintained with opponent

SPEAKING WITH SIGNS
This woman is a professional interpreter. Here, she translates the words being sung in an opera into sign language, so that hearing-impaired people in the audience can follow the opera's plot. Sign languages have been created by organizing gestures and signs into complete systems of communication.

AGGRESSION
Threatening body language has been studied in detail so that professionals can tell when violent behavior is likely, and attempt to avert it. Aggressive body language is, however, appropriate to some sports. This Japanese sumo wrestler adopts a typically aggressive pose to show that he is ready for the contest to begin.

BOREDOM
Body language and facial expressions are often subconscious forms of communication. We cannot help using them, even when there is nobody present to receive their messages. A slumped posture, head tilted to one side, and glazed expression are all obvious expressions of boredom.

Body tensed to spring

Hand covers mouth

THE LANGUAGE OF EXCITEMENT
Frequently, our body language reinforces exactly what we express in words. Wide eyes, an open mouth, and hands held together in a clapping position are all signs of excitement that would be difficult to miss.

SHOCK OR MOCK?
Exaggerated gestures need to be taken in context. This expression of horror could be a sincere reaction of shock to a violent act. On the other hand, it could simply be a gesture of mock horror in reaction to unwelcome news, such as extra homework for the weekend.

A GIVEAWAY
Sometimes our body language gives away certain truths that we are trying to hide. A hand in front of the mouth when talking can be a sign that the speaker is either lying or not telling the whole story. The liar may also find it difficult to maintain eye contact.

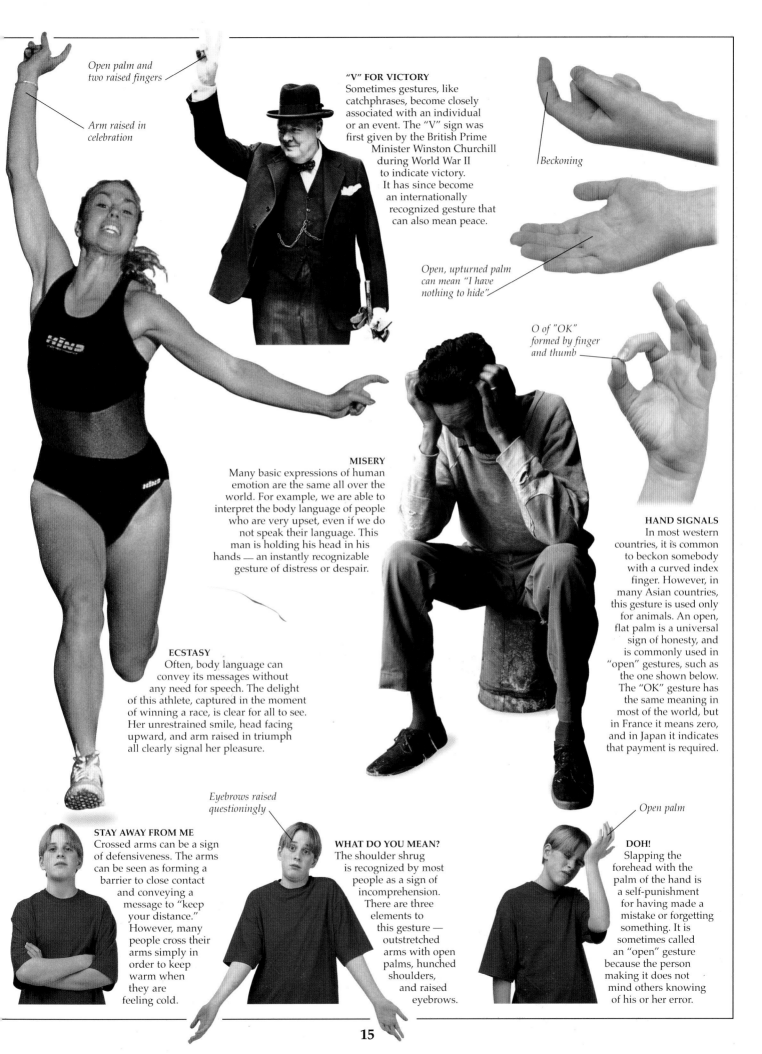

Open palm and two raised fingers

Arm raised in celebration

"V" FOR VICTORY
Sometimes gestures, like catchphrases, become closely associated with an individual or an event. The "V" sign was first given by the British Prime Minister Winston Churchill during World War II to indicate victory. It has since become an internationally recognized gesture that can also mean peace.

Beckoning

Open, upturned palm can mean "I have nothing to hide"

O of "OK" formed by finger and thumb

MISERY
Many basic expressions of human emotion are the same all over the world. For example, we are able to interpret the body language of people who are very upset, even if we do not speak their language. This man is holding his head in his hands — an instantly recognizable gesture of distress or despair.

HAND SIGNALS
In most western countries, it is common to beckon somebody with a curved index finger. However, in many Asian countries, this gesture is used only for animals. An open, flat palm is a universal sign of honesty, and is commonly used in "open" gestures, such as the one shown below. The "OK" gesture has the same meaning in most of the world, but in France it means zero, and in Japan it indicates that payment is required.

ECSTASY
Often, body language can convey its messages without any need for speech. The delight of this athlete, captured in the moment of winning a race, is clear for all to see. Her unrestrained smile, head facing upward, and arm raised in triumph all clearly signal her pleasure.

Eyebrows raised questioningly

Open palm

STAY AWAY FROM ME
Crossed arms can be a sign of defensiveness. The arms can be seen as forming a barrier to close contact and conveying a message to "keep your distance." However, many people cross their arms simply in order to keep warm when they are feeling cold.

WHAT DO YOU MEAN?
The shoulder shrug is recognized by most people as a sign of incomprehension. There are three elements to this gesture — outstretched arms with open palms, hunched shoulders, and raised eyebrows.

DOH!
Slapping the forehead with the palm of the hand is a self-punishment for having made a mistake or forgetting something. It is sometimes called an "open" gesture because the person making it does not mind others knowing of his or her error.

The story of writing

Stylus was pressed onto a clay tablet

BEFORE THE WRITTEN WORD EVOLVED, there was no way of permanently recording language. But as human knowledge expanded, the need for a system that stored information became more necessary. The first writing systems originated independently in China, Central America, and the Middle East, and were pictographic, which means that they used pictures to represent objects. These early systems were slow and could not convey abstract concepts, such as ideas and emotions. Gradually, as language developed, "true," or phonetic, alphabets evolved. These used letters and symbols to represent sounds instead of objects, and each sound made up part of a word.

Brush tip probably made from wolf hair

CUNEIFORM WRITING
The first consistent use of writing was practiced by the Sumerian culture in Mesopotamia (now Iraq). They developed a system called cuneiform, which used pictograms to represent the sounds of an object's name. Cuneiform was eventually used to record a number of Middle Eastern languages, and it continued to be used for over 3,000 years.

Chinese Ming calligraphy brush

Papyrus stems, used for making paper

Hieroglyphic sign is the word for "scribe"

Roman scribe holding a wax tablet

EGYPTIAN SCRIBE
This statue shows an ancient Egyptian scribe (professional writer). Scribes enjoyed high status, as very few people could read and write. This was not surprising, because ancient Egyptian writing, called hieroglyphs, was very complicated. There were over 700 different symbols, as well as two versions of the hieroglyphic script.

Amenhotep, an Egyptian scribe

Chinese ink block

Ancient Greek stylus

Roman stylus

WAXING LYRICAL
Ancient Greeks and Romans used a sharp writing implement called a stylus to etch writing into wax tablets. Writing was practiced by wealthy merchants and other members of the privileged middle classes for recording details of business transactions and for private letters.

CHINESE CALLIGRAPHY
The art of beautiful writing, known as calligraphy, requires years of practice using especially fine brushes, such as the one above. Calligraphy is considered an art form, and in China it is called one of the "three perfections," along with poetry and painting.

TYPEWRITING
The first practical typewriter appeared in 1867, and by the 1920s these machines were being used in offices in many parts of the world. Typewriting allowed clear, legible written communication to be performed much more quickly than writing by hand. Handwriting rarely exceeds a speed of 20 words per minute, but a trained typist can reach speeds of up to 120 words per minute.

"Bird" – early Sumerian
c. 3500 B.C.

"Bird" – Cuneiform
c. 3000 B.C.

"Bird" – Hieroglyphs
c. 3000 B.C.

"Bird" – Hebrew
c. 800 B.C.

Feather quill

Steel-nib pen

Fountain pen
and ink dropper

Disposable
ballpoint pen

"Bird" – Chinese
20th century

"Bird" – Braille
20th century

FROM FEATHERS TO STEEL
Pens made of dried and cleaned feathers were used from c. 500 B.C. The feather's hollow shaft, called a quill, contained ink that flowed out of a small split in the quill's sharpened point. Many famous writers, including Shakespeare, wrote their plays and novels with quill pens. In the 18th century, the steel-nib pen was introduced, but this still required the writer to dip the pen into an ink pot every few words.

MODERN IMPLEMENTS
The fountain pen was the first writing device to contain its own supply of ink. The pen was refilled from an inkwell, using a dropper; this arrangement was later replaced by easily inserted ink cartridges. The ballpoint pen, which appeared in 1938, offered cleaner writing with a constant ink flow and signaled the end of the fountain pen's reign. In 1950, the disposable ballpoint pen was invented.

CHANGING ALPHABETS
Above are some examples of the word "bird" in different scripts, showing how language has developed over time and place. Pictographic writing systems, such as cuneiform and Egyptian hieroglyphics, were eventually overtaken by true alphabets. The Braille alphabet, devised by Louis Braille (1809–1852) for blind people, is composed of groups of raised dots that represent different letters, and is read by touch.

Communicating with pictures

"ONE PICTURE IS WORTH a thousand words," goes an old saying, and this has been true throughout history. Pictures have been an ever-present and important part of communication since ancient times. Pictures can, in many cases, get across information that is too detailed or complex to be easily delivered in words. Some pictures and works of art are created simply to be pleasant to look at, but many do more than just this — they show an element of the culture and life of the time, tell a complete story, or offer warnings, instructions, or viewpoints about particular actions or events.

POLAROID PROOF
Photographs can be used to communicate important, up-to-date information. For example, instant photographs can be used by captors to show that their hostages are still alive. In the Polaroid above, a current newspaper is shown to prove that the victim is still alive.

STORYTELLING ART
Historians can learn much about the mythology (storytelling) of ancient cultures from surviving images. This ancient Greek vase shows a scene from the story of the twelve labors of Herakles, or Hercules. The Greek hero holds a giant boar above King Eurystheus, who cowers in a vase.

COMMENTING ON POLITICS
Political cartoons seek to make a point about politics and politicians of the day. This example by the political cartoonist James Gillray (1757–1815) shows caricatures of the British prime minister William Pitt (1759–1806) and the French leader Napoleon Bonaparte (1769–1821) dividing up the world between them.

Leaders of France and Great Britain carve up the globe

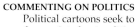

CARTOON HUMOR
Often, the purpose of a cartoon is simply to make people laugh or smile, but it can also be used to inform or make a specific point. In magazines, journals, and newspapers, cartoons, such as this one from the satirical magazine *Punch*, entertain and amuse the reader.

WOVEN HISTORY
The Bayeux tapestry is a perfect example of how an ancient artifact can give us a greater knowledge of important historical events. In dozens of finely woven scenes, it shows in great detail the events leading up to the Battle of Hastings (1066), in which the Norman prince, William the Conqueror, defeated King Harold, the Anglo-Saxon ruler of most of England.

This figure, who may be King Harold, is attempting to remove an arrow from his eye

A scene from the 11th-century Bayeux tapestry showing the death of King Harold

MORALITY PAINTING
This is a detail from a picture called *Netherlandish Proverbs*, which was painted in 1559 by the Dutch painter Pieter Brueghel the Elder. It contains many moral lessons, which often illustrate particular proverbs (sayings or words of guidance) of the time. The painting shows people how best to conduct their lives by illustrating the unhappy results of wrongdoing as well as examples of correct behavior.

These two women are spreading malicious gossip

A cheating wife places the cloak of deceit over her trusting husband's head

This man is filling in the pool after his calf has drowned in it — "too little, too late"

This figure is shearing a pig — a futile task because pigs have very little hair. The scene illustrates a popular proverb that points out the absurdity of much human behavior

This man represents wisdom because "the world turns on his thumb"

Halley's comet was considered by the Saxons to be a terrible omen

Bayeux tapestry scene showing the arrival of Halley's comet

King Harold sits on his throne in his palace

A messenger tells King Harold of the arrival of the comet in the sky

✳ Finding your way

ONE OF THE MAIN functions of communication is to provide help and instruction to others, and one of the most basic types of instruction is showing how to get from one place to another. Since earliest times, people have explored their surroundings and sought to find out more about the world. These travelers and explorers wanted to share the knowledge gained on their journeys, as well as purely practical information about the routes they used. At first, simple symbols, trail markings, and other route signs were used. As people learned more about the world around them, they were able to develop and communicate more sophisticated methods of navigation, and the science of cartography (mapmaking) became very important.

FOLLOWING THE STARS
These figures are representations of the three kings, or wise men, following the star of Bethlehem to reach the baby Jesus. The science of astronomy (charting the position of the stars) became useful for early travelers, who relied on certain stars for navigation. Although many navigational aids are now available, some people still use the stars to help them find their way.

Native American tracker

SIGNALING TO AIRCRAFT
International symbols are used for signaling to aircraft in emergencies. They can be constructed easily from large sticks or other found materials. The signs can ask for vital advice on where to proceed, and request further help or lifesaving supplies.

Traveling this way — follow

Safe to land here

Indicate correct direction to proceed

Sign made from sticks

Need compass and map

TRACKING THE WAY
Because of their nomadic lifestyle, many Native Americans were expert at navigating large areas of land. The new settlers from Europe used this skill when they started mapping areas of the New World in the 18th century. The settlers often employed Native Americans as trackers, and together they successfully mapped huge areas of the continent.

STONE MARKERS
Many cultures have used stones to show a path or trail ahead. Even today, piles of stones, called cairns, are used in parts of rural Europe to show walkers the correct route. Native Americans also used carefully arranged stones to indicate a change in direction.

Turn to the left

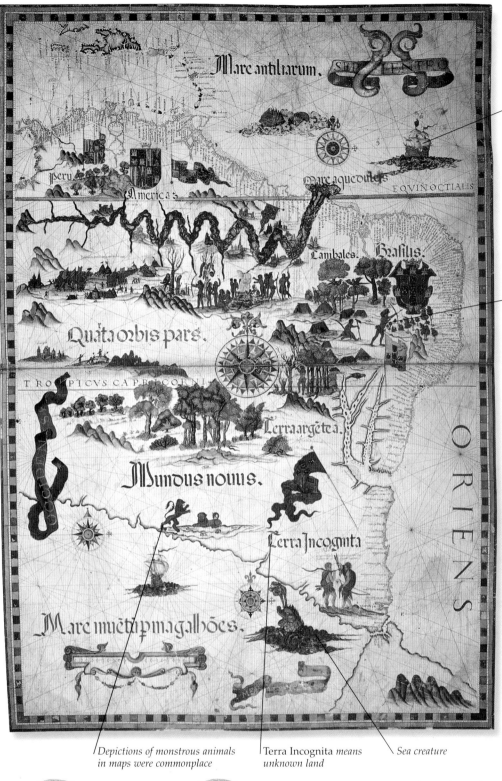

Mare antiliarum.

SEPTENTRIO

Peru

America

Mare aquedulcis

EQVINOCTIALIS

Cambales.

Brasilis.

Quarta orbis pars.

TROPICVS CAPRICORNI

Terra argentea.

Mundus nouus.

Terra Incognita

O R I E N S

Mare mueti pmagalhões.

Explorers'
ship

Needle
points
north

Indian
settlement

CHINESE KNOW-HOW
These 19th-century compasses
come from the Chinese port of
Canton. The magnetic compass —
with the needle always pointing
north — was invented by the
ancient Chinese. By the end of the
14th century, explorers all over the
world used it to calculate positions.

MAPPING PROGRESS
This map of South America was created
in 1558 by the Portuguese mapmaker
Diogo Homem. Originally employed by
the king of Portugal, Homem later sold
his skills to the English and Venetians.
Columbus's voyage to America in 1492
had provoked a geographic craze in
Europe, and cartographic skills and
knowledge were very highly prized.

Depictions of monstrous animals
in maps were commonplace

Terra Incognita *means*
unknown land

Sea creature

Continue
on this
path

Turn to
the right

NAVIGATING THE CITY
Today, people have to navigate
complicated routes through busy
cities. This modern traveler is
consulting a map showing all
the routes and stations of the
Paris Metro (subway) in
France. The map has been
carefully designed to
communicate information
quickly and clearly.

Postal systems

COMMUNICATION IS SUCCESSFUL ONLY if a message reaches its intended recipient, who may be a long distance away. From ancient Egyptian times, postal systems based on relaying messages by foot or horseback were used to keep rulers and nobles in touch with their empires. Private and public postal systems subsequently developed in many countries, as increasing numbers of people learned to read and write, especially after the invention of the printed book. These postal systems were expensive, and the cost of transporting a letter was usually paid for by the recipient. The 19th century saw a boom in affordable public postal systems. In 1789, there were just 75 post offices in the United States. By 1901, this number had increased to a massive 77,000.

MEDIEVAL MESSENGER
This 15th-century illustration shows the Sire de Rochechouart receiving a message from the king of France. Throughout the Middle Ages, messengers were used to ferry communications between rulers and their generals and nobles. Messengers were costly and could be afforded only by the very wealthy.

News of Lincoln's election as president, carried by Pony Express

POSTAL CARRIAGE
As the amount of public mail increased, postal services started to use mail coaches, such as this one, built in the 1780s. Highwaymen posed a constant threat to mail coaches, and people were advised to cut paper money in two and send the two halves in separate letters or packages. With the advent of the railroads, the use of mail coaches declined.

PONY EXPRESS
The famous Pony Express of 1860–1861 used relays of fast riders on horseback. They rode from St. Joseph, Missouri to Sacramento, California — a distance of over 1,864 miles (3,000 km). Changing horses every 10–15 miles (16–24 km), these riders took between 10 and 16 days to deliver mail — the fastest post system until the cross-country telegraph was established.

PENNY BLACK
Britain was the first country to introduce a system for pre-payment of postage on letters. In 1840, the government made the cost of sending a letter one penny. Proof of payment was supplied by a small black sticker with Queen Victoria's head on it. This was the first postage stamp, the now famous and highly collectible "penny black."

The coach driver sat here and kept a constant lookout for highwaymen, who were attracted by the possibility of money and valuables

| Letter posted in city mailbox | Mail sorted into destination regions | Transported by land and air | Arrives at main sorting office | Travels to island on a mail boat | Letter delivered to personal mailbox |

Air mail letter

THE JOURNEY OF A LETTER

We take it for granted when we mail a letter that it will reach its destination, even if this is on a remote island. The process actually involves large numbers of people and many different means of transportation. Letters have to be first sorted into destination regions, then transported there, and finally sorted into local areas, ready for postal workers to deliver.

POSTCARDS

The postcard was invented in 1861 by a Philadelphia man, John P. Charlton, who sold the rights to a local stationer, Harry L. Lipman. Lipman published postcards with an appealing picture on one side and space to write the address and a short message on the other. Today, millions of postcards are sent every year, especially by vacationers.

AIRMAIL BY ZEPPELIN

Transporting mail by air began in 1911, allowing letters to cross seas and oceans in a fraction of the time it took by ship. This picture commemorates the arrival of a German zeppelin airship in Tokyo in 1929, after a 12-day round-the-world flight.

THE MAILMEN

In Britain over 200 years ago, mail was often delivered by children on horseback. They had to work in all weather, and were often attacked by highwaymen. If they were robbed, or if they carried illegal mail, they could be sentenced to hard labor. The biggest threat to today's letter carriers is aggressive dogs!

French mailbox

PUBLIC MAILBOXES

The famous British novelist Anthony Trollope (1815–1882) was also a surveyor for the Post Office, and was responsible for the first national network of public mailboxes in 1853. Soon, mailboxes were being used in many countries; they appeared in U.S. city streets in 1858. They did not catch on right away, as people were wary of leaving their personal letters in a box in the street all day.

U.S. mailbox

Words in print

BEFORE BOOKS, written language was confined to a few stone and clay tablets and parchment scrolls. It was not until books became available that written language had a major impact on communication. For centuries, books were rare and expensive. Each one was handwritten by monks or scribes, a process that took many months. Today, a modern printing press can produce thousands of copies of a book in one day. Many books are now lightweight, portable, and cheap. The book has survived competition from recent media, such as television and computers, and remains a vital method of communication.

DIAMOND SUTRA
This Buddhist scroll, called the Diamond Sutra, is probably the oldest printed book in the world. It was printed in 868 A.D. using carved wooden blocks, a system invented by the Chinese in the 6th century. Each block took a long time to carve and could be used only for that particular book. Even so, woodblock printing was far quicker than copying by hand (the method used in Europe until the 1450s) when more than one copy of a work was required.

Cover of the Lindisfarne Gospels

Gemstones decorate the cover

Digital manuscripts

An exciting new project at London's British Library uses the very latest technology to make ancient manuscripts accessible to the public. Many very old books are too rare and valuable to be handled — they need to be kept safely under lock and key. Some of these rare books, including the Lindisfarne Gospels, have been scanned into an advanced computer system. This system has been designed to enable readers to touch, read, and examine these beautiful relics of another age without any danger of damaging them.

Electronic pages of the Lindisfarne Gospels

Before the arrival of books in great numbers, it was much easier for rulers to control what people thought. Books often challenge existing systems by providing new ideas. The power of books has often resulted in their mass destruction. This burning of Chinese books was by anti-Chinese demonstrators in Taiwan.

BOOKS FOR ALL
These Penguin books, published in 1935, were among the first paperback books. Before their publication, only expensive hardback books were sold, which some people could not afford. The new, cheap paperbacks helped improve reading skills and made great literature available to everyone.

TURNING THE PAGES
It is possible to flick through the electronic version of the Lindisfarne Gospels just as you would a real book. The exhibit's ingenious touchscreen registers the finger at the corner of the page, and then runs a realistic computer animation of a page turning before displaying the next one.

Hand-drawn details, called illuminations

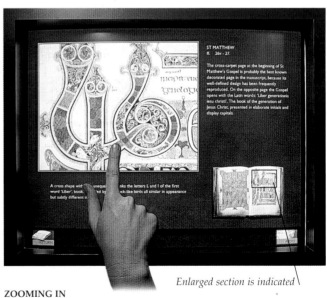

Enlarged section is indicated

ZOOMING IN
Because the manuscript is permanently held in the computer's memory, it is possible to zoom in and out at the touch of a finger. Zooming in allows the user to see the richness and intricacy of the Lindisfarne Gospels' detail. Part of the screen is sometimes used to display helpful information about the book.

The power of the press

IN THE DEVELOPED WORLD, most adults read some form of newspaper regularly, and newspapers can have a great influence on public opinion. Powerful newspaper owners frequently try to affect the way that events are reported. Most newspapers have particular viewpoints, and journalists may choose to slant stories to reflect these outlooks. Some may even go as far as altering photographs to make events suit their own purposes. And almost all newspapers treat the achievements of their own country as especially important.

THE NEWS IN 1912
Before the arrival of radio, newsreels, and television, major events, such as the tragic tale of the sinking of the *Titanic* in 1912, left, were brought to the world by newspapers alone.

Georgi Malenkov

Signing the treaty of peace in 1950, after WWII

Headline interprets the space flight as a great victory for socialism

Letter of congratulation to Gagarin from Soviet leader Khruschev

СОВЕТСКИЙ ЧЕЛОВЕК В КОСМОСЕ!

ЮРИЙ ГАГАРИН: ПРОШУ ДОЛОЖИТЬ ПАРТИИ И ПРАВИТЕЛЬСТВУ И ЛИЧНО НИКИТЕ СЕРГЕЕВИЧУ ХРУЩЕВУ, ЧТО ПРИЗЕМЛЕНИЕ ПРОШЛО НОРМАЛЬНО, ЧУВСТВУЮ СЕБЯ ХОРОШО

ВЕЛИЧАЙШАЯ ПОБЕДА НАШЕГО СТРОЯ, НАШЕЙ НАУКИ, НАШЕЙ ТЕХНИКИ, НАШЕГО МУЖЕСТВА
12 АПРЕЛЯ 1961 ГОДА В 10 ЧАСОВ 55 МИНУТ КОСМИЧЕСКИЙ КОРАБЛЬ-СПУТНИК «ВОСТОК» БЛАГОПОЛУЧНО ВЕРНУЛСЯ НА СВЯЩЕННУЮ ЗЕМЛЮ НАШЕЙ РОДИНЫ

ИЗВЕСТИЯ
СОВЕТОВ ДЕПУТАТОВ ТРУДЯЩИХСЯ СССР

Четверг, 13 апреля 1961 г.

СОВЕТСКОМУ КОСМОНАВТУ, ВПЕРВЫЕ В МИРЕ СОВЕРШИВШЕМУ КОСМИЧЕСКИЙ ПОЛЕТ
Майору Гагарину Юрию Алексеевичу

ВСЕМ УЧЕНЫМ, ИНЖЕНЕРАМ, ТЕХНИКАМ, РАБОЧИМ, ВСЕМ КОЛЛЕКТИВАМ И ОРГАНИЗАЦИЯМ, УЧАСТВОВАВШИМ В УСПЕШНОМ ОСУЩЕСТВЛЕНИИ ПЕРВОГО В МИРЕ КОСМИЧЕСКОГО ПОЛЕТА ЧЕЛОВЕКА НА КОРАБЛЕ-СПУТНИКЕ «ВОСТОК» ПЕРВОМУ СОВЕТСКОМУ КОСМОНАВТУ ТОВАРИЩУ ГАГАРИНУ ЮРИЮ АЛЕКСЕЕВИЧУ

О ПЕРВОМ В МИРЕ ПОЛЕТЕ ЧЕЛОВЕКА В КОСМИЧЕСКОЕ ПРОСТРАНСТВО
СООБЩЕНИЕ ТАСС

DOCTORING PHOTOGRAPHS
Many Soviet and Chinese officials, including Joseph Stalin and Mao Zedong, the leaders of the U.S.S.R. and China, were present at the signing of the treaty of peace. However, according to the picture above, published in a Soviet national newspaper in 1953, only Stalin, Mao, and Malenkov were present. The other officials had been removed to make Malenkov seem more important than he really was.

Picture of Yuri Gagarin dominates front page

Report from the landing place

FRONT PAGE, SOVIET-STYLE
On April 12 1961, the Soviet cosmonaut Yuri Gagarin became the first man in space. The U.S.A. and U.S.S.R. had been involved in a "space race" since 1957, and this event was a great triumph for the Soviet Union. The story took up the national newspaper *Izvestiya*'s entire front page. The paper covered all aspects of the event, including a description of the flight, a report from the landing place, and a history of the Soviet Union's space program.

THE SUNDAY PAPERS

The circulation of newspapers has declined since the 1950s as more and more people get their news from radio and television. Some newspapers have attempted to win readers by becoming more like magazines. The sober, thin (London) *Sunday Times* on the left is from 1958, when only political and sporting events were suitable subjects for a national newspaper. The one on the right is from 1999 and boasts no fewer than 11 separate sections, covering many different topics ranging from book and film reviews to travel and fashion.

In the 1950s, serious newspapers had few pictures and used small print

Photograph of the trial of a former Nazi has been chosen over one of Gagarin

Entire section devoted to fashion

The New York Times.

"All the News That's Fit to Print"

LATE CITY EDITION

VOL. CX. No. 37,699.

NEW YORK, WEDNESDAY, APRIL 12, 1961.

FIVE CENTS

SOVIET ORBITS MAN AND RECOVERS HIM; SPACE PIONEER REPORTS: 'I FEEL WELL'; SENT MESSAGES WHILE CIRCLING EARTH

HEAD OF RESERVE URGES PRICE CUTS TO RELIEVE SLUMP

Martin Asserts Reductions Would Mean More Jobs and Demand for Goods

Wide College Aid Is Adopted by State

ISRAEL DEFENDS TRIBUNAL'S RIGHT TO TRY EICHMANN

Ex-Nazi Is More Confident as Jerusalem Hearing Enters Its 2d Day

Former Nazi Hears Indictment Read as Trial Begins in Jerusalem

187-MILE HEIGHT

Yuri Gagarin, a Major, Makes the Flight in 5-Ton Vehicle

Adolf Eichmann, charged with crimes against the Jewish people and against humanity, standing in special booth in Beit Haam courtroom yesterday. Justices at bench are, from left, Benjamin Halevi, Moshe Landau, Yitzhak Raveh.

COUNCIL APPROVES OWN CHARTER BILL

U. S. IS DISTURBED BY DELAY ON LAO.

Soviet Lag on Cease-Fire and Increase in Supplies Regarded as Ominous

Eichmann peers intently at tribunal during proceedings

FRANCE DECLARES ANTI-'U.N. STRIKE'

De Gaulle Bars Any Role in Armed Ventures—Warns Algerians on Partition

BRITISH CONSIDER TRADE UNITY STEP

Kennedy Hopes London Will Enter Common Market

ADENAUER IN U.S. TO SEE KENNEDY

Arrives for First Talks With President—Stresses Unity

Population Center Moves West; Census Puts It at Centralia, Ill.

Realtor Is Indicted In Expense Padding

Centennial of War Rocked by Dispute

White House Confirms Firing; Feat Hailed by U. S. Scientists

NEWS INDEX

209

Just one column out of eight is devoted to the space flight

Supporting story focuses on U.S. space tracking stations

TODAY'S VARIETY

Publishing a national newspaper is an expensive business, but the cost of producing a special-interest magazine has plummeted. The use of computers and desktop publishing software has made it possible to produce small numbers of a publication and still make a profit. As a result, it is now possible to buy magazines featuring such unlikely subjects as coiled wire, collecting phone cards, and breeding budgerigars.

FRONT PAGE, AMERICAN-STYLE

The front page of *The New York Times* on April 12, 1961, was very different from *Izvestiya*. Although the Soviet Union's space flight is the main story, it jostles for space on the page with many others, and there is no photograph of Yuri Gagarin. The reporter has kept to the bare facts of the story, which are related in a low-key tone. The first man in space was an event of worldwide significance — but it was a political triumph only for the Soviet Union.

27

The first telecommunications

IN 1876, WITH THE WORDS "Mr. Watson, come here, I want you," Alexander Graham Bell (1847–1922) ushered in the start of a revolutionary new form of communication — the telephone — that was to have an enormous impact on people's everyday lives. However, the telephone was not the first telecommunications ("tele" means long distance) machine. That title belongs to the telegraph, which began its practical life in the 1830s. Many forms of telegraphs and early telephones used radio or electrical signals to carry information along an electrical wire, and different strengths of current could be used to represent letters of the alphabet or speech. When the telephone was first introduced, instructions had to be issued explaining how to use it. Initially, people either were struck dumb or shouted down the telephone.

UNDERSEA CABLE
Above is a fragment of the undersea telecommunications cable that was laid in the English Channel in 1891 to link France and the United Kingdom. Telephone signals traveled along copper wiring housed inside the thick protective covering.

GOWER-BELL TELEPHONE
The Gower-Bell telephone (right), made in 1881, was used by a number of early telephone services. The British Post Office converted its small public telegraph exchange to use this phone. In 1890, Gower-Bell telephones were also used to construct the first telephone service for practical use in Japan, between Tokyo and Yokohama.

Caller speaks into this mouthpiece

Earpieces are attached to tubes, which are hooked to the telephone when not in use

Transmitter and receiver are housed in the body of the telephone

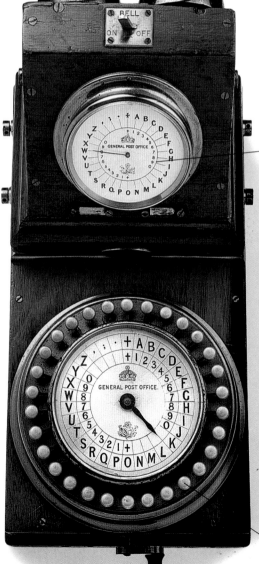

This dial recorded the last transmitted letter

TELEGRAMS AND TOKENS
For public use, telegraphed messages were printed or written out on paper. These messages were called telegrams. Special tokens were used instead of money to pay telegraph messengers for replies to telegrams they had delivered.

ABC TELEGRAPH
The British inventor Charles Wheatstone built the first ABC telegraph in 1848. Messages were sent by pulses that moved a needle around a clock face, the pauses of the needle spelling out the message. The machine (left) was slow but very easy to operate and soon became widely used by post offices in the United Kingdom.

Messages were transmitted letter by letter using these buttons

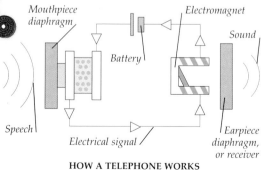

Mouthpiece diaphragm

Electromagnet

Sound

Battery

Speech

Electrical signal

Earpiece diaphragm, or receiver

HOW A TELEPHONE WORKS
Sound travels in waves, which vibrate a flexible disk, or diaphragm, in the telephone mouthpiece. The diaphragm turns sound into electrical signals. These pass down the phone line to the earpiece. Then an electromagnet converts the signals back into sound.

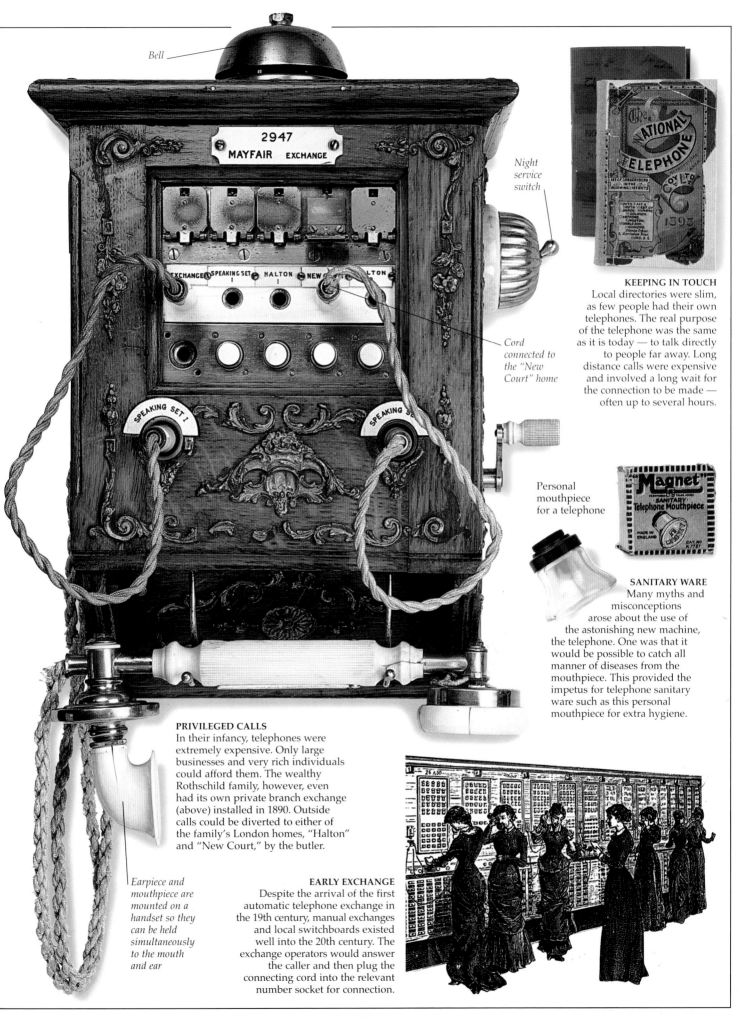

Bell

2947
MAYFAIR EXCHANGE

Night service switch

Cord connected to the "New Court" home

SPEAKING SET 1

SPEAKING S

KEEPING IN TOUCH
Local directories were slim, as few people had their own telephones. The real purpose of the telephone was the same as it is today — to talk directly to people far away. Long distance calls were expensive and involved a long wait for the connection to be made — often up to several hours.

Personal mouthpiece for a telephone

SANITARY WARE
Many myths and misconceptions arose about the use of the astonishing new machine, the telephone. One was that it would be possible to catch all manner of diseases from the mouthpiece. This provided the impetus for telephone sanitary ware such as this personal mouthpiece for extra hygiene.

PRIVILEGED CALLS
In their infancy, telephones were extremely expensive. Only large businesses and very rich individuals could afford them. The wealthy Rothschild family, however, even had its own private branch exchange (above) installed in 1890. Outside calls could be diverted to either of the family's London homes, "Halton" and "New Court," by the butler.

Earpiece and mouthpiece are mounted on a handset so they can be held simultaneously to the mouth and ear

EARLY EXCHANGE
Despite the arrival of the first automatic telephone exchange in the 19th century, manual exchanges and local switchboards existed well into the 20th century. The exchange operators would answer the caller and then plug the connecting cord into the relevant number socket for connection.

Telecommunications today

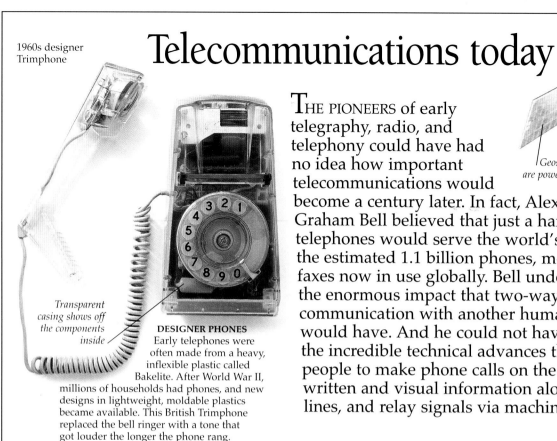

Transparent casing shows off the components inside

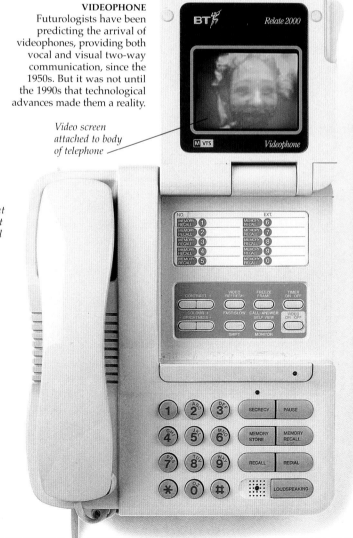

Geostationary satellites are powered by solar panels

THE PIONEERS of early telegraphy, radio, and telephony could have had no idea how important telecommunications would become a century later. In fact, Alexander Graham Bell believed that just a handful of telephones would serve the world's needs — not the estimated 1.1 billion phones, modems, and faxes now in use globally. Bell underestimated the enormous impact that two-way, direct communication with another human voice would have. And he could not have predicted the incredible technical advances that allow people to make phone calls on the move, send written and visual information along phone lines, and relay signals via machines in space.

DESIGNER PHONES
Early telephones were often made from a heavy, inflexible plastic called Bakelite. After World War II, millions of households had phones, and new designs in lightweight, moldable plastics became available. This British Trimphone replaced the bell ringer with a tone that got louder the longer the phone rang.

Document prints out on arrival

FAX MACHINE
Since the 1960s, telephone lines have been used for sending important documents, maps, and drawings instantly. Fax machines scan the contents of a page, convert it into electronic pulses, and send these pulses along a telephone line. On arrival, the pulses are converted back to a printed page.

VIDEOPHONE
Futurologists have been predicting the arrival of videophones, providing both vocal and visual two-way communication, since the 1950s. But it was not until the 1990s that technological advances made them a reality.

Video screen attached to body of telephone

Each fiber is the thickness of a human hair

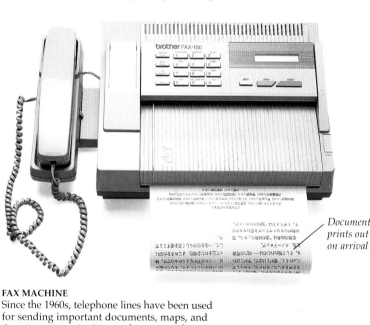

Protective covering

FIBER OPTICS
Traditional copper wiring is being fast replaced by optical fibers. These are fine threads of glass so pure that you could see perfectly through a 12-mile (20-km)-thick block of them. The telephone call's electrical signals travel down the fiber as infrared light. Unlike copper wiring, optical fibers carry thousands of signals at the same time without any interference.

SATELLITE PHONE

Portable telephones can now be linked to satellite systems so that calls can be made from absolutely anywhere in the world. This driver of a dogsled team on isolated Baffin Island, Canada, has an instant link to civilization with his portable phone.

Signal travels to ground station

SATELLITE SYSTEMS

About 150 communication satellites are in orbit around the Earth. They are called geostationary satellites because they travel at the same speed as the Earth — and so appear to be stationary. The satellites receive signals from transmitter dishes, amplify them, and relay them back to a ground station. In this way, the signals are transmitted to other continents, enabling instant worldwide telecommunication.

PAGERS

Pagers are small radio receivers that offer portable one-way communication. They are widely used by professional people, such as doctors, who need to be able to be contacted quickly wherever they are.

MOBILE PHONES

The first mobile telephones became available in about 1979. These phones use radio networks to transmit signals, so they can be used wherever there is a transmitter nearby. Since mobile phones have become relatively cheap and accessible, people use the telephone more than ever before.

Ground station receives signals from the satellite

The impact of radio

RADIO WAVES ARE A WAY of sending electrical signals over distances without wires or cables. Many scientists and engineers contributed to the development of wireless communication, and in 1895 the Italian physicist Guglielmo Marconi (1874–1937) made the first radio transmission. Marconi originally used radio waves to send telegraph messages, but he soon progressed to sending sound signals. At first, radio technology was confined to scientists and research establishments, but by the 1920s wealthy individuals were receiving the first public broadcasts on their own crystal radio sets. By the 1930s, people in many countries were hearing news, dramatizations, and performances from thousands of miles away. Radio had become the first mass broadcast media.

EARLY RECEIVER
This primitive radio receiver, or coherer, was invented by the French scientist Edouard Branly in 1890. It contains metal filings that act as a conductor for the current. The design was improved and adapted by Guglielmo Marconi and used in his pioneering transmissions.

National Broadcasting Corporation microphone

FIRESIDE CHATS
Some politicians were quick to exploit the potential power of broadcasting messages to an entire country. During the 1930s, President Franklin Roosevelt made regular broadcasts in which he spelled out new initiatives and policies. These "fireside chats," as they became known, reassured people and contributed to Roosevelt's popularity.

HOME ENTERTAINMENT
Radio was not just a way of providing immediate news; it was also an exciting new form of entertainment, and it grew quickly in popularity from the late 1920s onward. The variety shows, serials, and music recitals broadcast on radio became the focal point of many family evenings.

Children gathered around the radio

RADIO FOR ALL
Until the late 1920s, headphones were required for listening to the radio. This Gecophone, built in 1925, was the first publicly available radio set that amplified the sound enough for headphones not to be needed. This allowed people to listen to the radio together, making it a social occasion.

Horn helped to amplify, or increase, the volume of the sound signal

Stand to support horn

WAR OF THE WORLDS
In 1938, the American actor Orson Welles broadcast a dramatization of H.G. Wells's novel about a Martian invasion, *War of the Worlds*, on a U.S. network. Many listeners believed that it was a real newscast and that Martians had actually landed. Some, such as this man, even armed themselves for defense.

PIRATE RADIO
In Britain, radio licenses were not granted to commercial radio stations until the end of the 1960s. But pirate, or illegal, commercial stations such as Radio Caroline, above, went on the air before then, broadcasting offshore from boats and ships to avoid detection.

Instructions housed in box lid

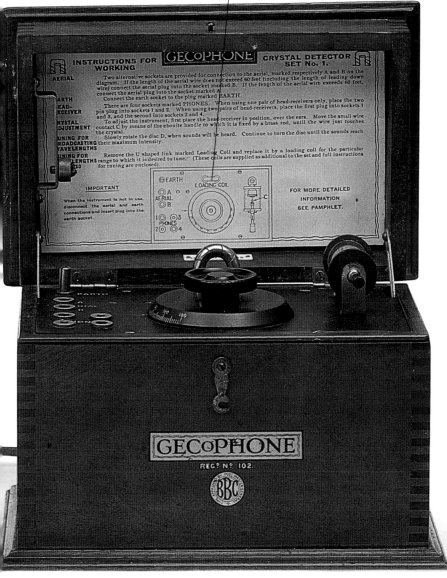

TWO-WAY RADIO
Radio was essentially a one-way broadcast medium until the arrival of the phone-in talk show in the 1960s. These shows encouraged listeners to phone in to air their views on particular subjects or to take part in competitions. Talk shows have grown in popularity and now cover all kinds of topics. This DJ in Cincinnati, Ohio, hosts a matchmaking program called *Desperate and Dateless*.

ENERGY SAVER
The invention of the transistor in the 1950s made cheaper and smaller radios possible. By the 1980s, it was possible to fit a radio inside a wristwatch, and a recent advance, digital radio, now promises CD-quality sound. This 1990s Baygen Freeplay radio offers a different technological breakthrough — it requires no batteries. Instead, an ingenious mechanism stores energy from just a few turns of the external handle.

The moving image

IN 1895, THE FIRST FILMS were projected in Paris by the Lumière brothers, French pioneers of early cinema. Less than a year later, cinemas had sprung up all over the world. A new chapter in mass broadcast media had begun — moving pictures, capable of informing, educating, and, above all, telling stories, had arrived, and the new medium reached huge numbers of people. Many of the early cinemas, nicknamed "picture palaces," had thousands of seats. Early films were silent, but by 1929 the "talkies" had appeared, and in 1935 the first color film was released.

NAUGHTY CINEMA
The first cinema was not the family affair it is today. Sequences of pictures were viewed, by one person at a time, on devices such as this Mutoscope, invented in 1894. Turning the handle flipped a series of cards portraying a mildly naughty scene.

NEWS ON FILM
In 1909, the French brothers Charles and Emile Pathé started to produce newsreel films, which were shown before the main feature. Their influence grew, and during World War II newsreels were vital in providing information about the progress of the war.

THE BRIGHTEST STAR
Charlie Chaplin (1889–1977) was the biggest star of cinema's silent era. Born in Britain, he emigrated to the U.S.A. in 1912, and within a few years he had achieved worldwide fame. His films are known for their empathy with ordinary people.

POPULARITY OF CINEMA
As television grew in popularity during the 1950s, the status of cinema diminished. The film industry tried to hold on to its customers by producing more extravagant blockbusters, as well as introducing gimmicks such as 3-D films, above. But audiences continued to dwindle until the 1980s. Now, moviegoing has regained its popularity, and the film industry is an ever-growing multibillion-dollar industry.

A line of moviegoers stretches into the distance

Magazines hold the three strips of film

Lightproof door closes when camera is running

GLORIOUS COLOR
In the 1920s, filmmakers attempted to mimic the real world of color by hand-tinting black-and-white film. In 1932, the invention of the Technicolor Three-Strip Camera (above) enabled real color filming. However, these cameras were prohibitively expensive and, even in the mid-1950s, half of all films were still made in black and white.

ESCAPE INTO CINEMA
Released in 1939, the U.S. fantasy film *The Wizard of Oz* proved irresistible to a world on the brink of World War II. The success of a film may depend on its ability to interpret the desires of the public — in this case a desire for escapism.

CHINESE CINEMA
The Chinese film industry initially tried to imitate Hollywood's lavish blockbusters. However, under communist rule, films that reflect Chinese philosophies, attitudes, and ways of life have been produced.

BOLLYWOOD
The Indian film industry, based in Bombay and known as Bollywood, produces more films than its U.S. counterpart, although few of them are released in the West. Indian films are often colorful combinations of musicals, love stories, and action adventures, such as the one advertised in the poster above.

FANTASY OR REALITY?
For many people, watching a film means becoming immersed in a fantasy world. Some filmmakers have played with this tendency to blur the boundaries between film and reality. In the 1993 U.S. film *The Last Action Hero,* Arnold Schwarzenegger, above, steps out of the screen into the theater itself.

CARTOON MEETS LIVE ACTION
By the 1980s, computer technology was advanced enough to be able to combine live-action cinema with cartoon animation. The 1988 U.S. film *Who Framed Roger Rabbit* was the first full-length feature to use this technique. By 1996, the film *Space Jam*, starring the basketball superstar Michael Jordan, right, and the vintage cartoon star Daffy Duck, was able to achieve slick, realistic results.

The television age

TELEVISION MADE A GREATER IMPACT on 20th-century life than any other medium. It started out in 1925, in the attic workshop of an amateur Scottish scientist, John Logie Baird (1888–1946). In 1926, Baird made the first television transmission, but his mechanical system was overtaken in 1929 when an American inventor, Vladimir Zworykin (1889–1982), built the first electronic television. In 1954, the first color broadcasts were made. Before long, television had overtaken movies as the main entertainment medium. For the first time, current events could be broadcast as they happened. In recent years, satellite, cable, and digital television have provided a wider choice of programs.

THE FIRST TELEVISION
In 1926, the Scottish inventor John Logie Baird developed a "visual wireless," the mechanical Televisor system, above. In 1930, it became available to the public. This early television had a tiny screen and was not capable of broadcasting sound and pictures together.

TV OWNERSHIP
This graph charts the rise of television ownership worldwide. There are around 997 million sets in use today. Although more than 95 percent of households in developed nations have one or more televisions, the figure is much lower for many other nations. In Afghanistan, for instance, less than one percent of households have a TV set.

Worldwide TV owners in millions

Year	1950	1960	1970	1980	1990

(Values on vertical axis: 1, 2, 3, 4, 5, 50, 100, 200, 400, 600, 800, 1,000)

EARLY VIEWING
The first regular television broadcasts came from the BBC (British Broadcasting Corporation) in 1936. Early television programming was an odd mixture of radio-style announcements, movie newsreels, and entertainments such as juggling. But gradually, outside broadcasts of live events, staged dramas, interviews, and debates were introduced.

THE NATION WATCHES
In 1963, President John F. Kennedy was assassinated in an open car in Dallas, Texas (left). The event was captured on a home movie and broadcast on TV around the world. For four days, TV stations suspended commercial programs to concentrate on the story. The nation watched as a series of incredible events unfolded on their television sets.

MURDER CAPTURED BY TV CAMERAS
Two days after Kennedy's assassination, the prime suspect, Lee Harvey Oswald, was shot dead in front of TV cameras as he was taken to the county jail. Television viewers, hoping to catch a glimpse of the man who shot the president, witnessed his brutal murder instead.

Gunman Jack Ruby shoots Lee Harvey Oswald on live TV

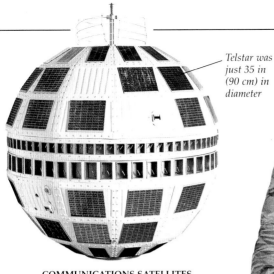

Telstar was just 35 in (90 cm) in diameter

Reflection of the lunar module in Aldrin's helmet

COMMUNICATIONS SATELLITES
In 1962, the satellite *Telstar* made history when it transmitted the first live TV pictures from the United States to Europe. *Telstar*'s low orbit hid it from transmitters and receivers, and it could operate for only a few hours a day. Today this problem is avoided because communications satellites rotate at the same speed as the Earth, and so seem to hold a stationary position.

PART OF THE FURNITURE
By the mid-1960s, the television's place in the living rooms of millions of homes was assured. Television design was subject to the fashions of the time. This 1970 JVC Videosphere was shaped like an astronaut's helmet to mirror the interest in space travel.

LIVE FROM THE MOON
On July 20, 1969, 723 million people — a quarter of the world's population — tuned in to watch the astronaut Neil Armstrong make his "giant leap for mankind" by walking on the moon. Live television pictures were transmitted an incredible distance of 239,000 miles (385,000 km), helping to secure television's status as the medium of the future.

A video-CD

GOING DIGITAL
Television technology is constantly advancing; there are now television sets so small you can hold them in your hand (below). Programs can be recorded and watched on videotape and on video-CD. More recently, HD (high definition) TV and digital TV offer higher-quality images and greater choice of channels.

People had to sit close to the television because of the small screen

Astronaut Edwin "Buzz" Aldrin, photographed on the moon by Neil Armstrong

The French captain, Zinedine Zidane, lifts World Cup trophy

France wins the 1998 World Cup

A MASS AUDIENCE
Today television has become a truly global medium. While countries and regions have their own programming, some events — from major political scandals to sporting contests such as the Olympics and soccer's World Cup — attract a worldwide audience. The 64 games that made up the 1998 World Cup, held in France, were watched by a total worldwide audience of 37 billion.

Making news

SOME EVENTS, such as wars, natural disasters, and serious crimes, become major news stories and are always reported widely by newspapers, radio, television, and the Internet. But there is often a demand for unusual, small-scale tales that appeal to human emotions. Sometimes, a local story is picked up by national newspapers and television and even becomes international news. When this happens, a modest event can snowball to involve a large media network, from local reporters to international news corporations. This was the case with the tale of two pigs that saved their bacon when they escaped from their owner in Malmesbury, Wiltshire, England, in 1998.

1 THE OWNER'S TALE
In January 1998, two Ginger Tamworth boars escaped from their owner, farmer Arnoldo Dijulio (above), on their way to the slaughterhouse. By the time they were recaptured, the pigs had become so famous that Mr. Dijulio was able to sell them for $24,000 to a national newspaper. Had he sold them at the slaughterhouse, they would have fetched $128.

2 THE LOCAL NEWS
Local reporters are often on the lookout for strange or funny events in their own areas. When the Tamworth pigs escaped, local journalists wasted no time in investigating the event. Usually, when a newsworthy event takes place, a local reporter, often accompanied by a photographer, is sent out to obtain details and quotes from eyewitnesses in order to put the full story together.

In the dead of night, a member of the public tries to grab one of the pigs

3 NATIONAL PRESS
The story of the two pigs, now nicknamed the Tamworth Two, appeared in the national press. Newspapers, such as *The Daily Mail*, right, set out to capture public attention by writing and headlining the story in an entertaining way, and by going over details of the event as if it were serious news. The British public loved the story of the two escaped pigs. Animal sanctuaries volunteered to give the pair a home for life, and offers of cash came in from all over England.

The Grunt Escape

On the run, pigs who saved themselves from getting the pork chop

Boys see 'tiger' in woods

Map detailing the pigs' escape route

4 PUBLIC INTEREST
When a story arouses public interest, news media respond by running more features and follow-up stories linked to the subject. Sometimes, media attention can itself become the news. News teams from Europe and the United States came to report on the British media's surprising interest in the story, rather than the actual tale of the two fugitive pigs.

5 ELECTRONIC NEWS GATHERING
Interest in the story grew, and more news crews descended on the little town of Malmesbury. Some television news teams use electronic news gathering (ENG) units, which have their own video editing facilities. Relevant material is recorded on videotape using lightweight, portable cameras, and edited right away. Using this system, entire reports are put together on site, and are then transported to the newsroom by portable radio transmitter.

6 INTERNATIONAL PRESS
Lighthearted stories, such as this one, prove especially popular when much of the international news is gloomy. Before long, the story of the runaway pigs and the media interest in them had made the news in much of Europe, in Japan, and in New Zealand.

Nose-mounted camera can swivel 360°

Squirrel AS355-F1 helicopter used for news gathering

7 NEWS HELICOPTER
Britain's ITN (Independent Television News) helicopter visited Malmesbury and sent back video and still pictures to the newsroom. This helicopter is the only aircraft in Europe permanently equipped for television news gathering and transmission.

8 NATIONAL NEWSROOM
News gathered by reporters is fed to the newsroom, where it is edited to fit bulletins. Editors have to choose which stories to feature, for how long, and in what order. They may mix film footage from libraries, prerecorded interviews, and on-the-spot reports compiled by ENG teams.

9 REGULAR BROADCASTS
Reading from a screen called an autoscript, which is out of view, this BBC newscaster gives a national television broadcast. The story of the Tamworth Two was featured regularly as the final news bulletin for a whole week.

10 NEWS SATELLITES
Many of the reports made by foreign news crews covering the Tamworth Two were sent around the world by satellite. This Intelsat 7-series satellite can transmit three television channels and thousands of phone lines simultaneously.

The pigs devour an anniversary cake

11 INTERNATIONAL TV COVERAGE
The U.S. broadcasting channel NBC sent a film crew to Malmesbury to report on the Tamworth Two. Their story was sent back via satellite to the NBC newsroom in the United States, and it was featured as a news bulletin.

12 ONE YEAR LATER
In 1999, the two pigs enjoyed an anniversary party held in their honor. They are living proof of how newsmaking can create celebrities — even out of pigs! The two have been called upon to appear in public, and furry toy Tamworth Two pigs have been produced.

Advertising

ADVERTISING USES COMMUNICATIONS media to promote the sale of goods and services, and to project a company's image. Modern advertising started in the 19th-century United States when businesses found that the best way to reach people living in far-flung areas was to send out catalogs promoting their wares. Over time, advertisers have learned the art of persuading people to buy. Many modern advertisements apply basic psychology by appealing to people's insecurities and desires. And as advertising becomes more sophisticated, it is more wide-ranging; for example, brand-name products are "placed" in feature films and endorsed by celebrities, and theater plays, TV shows, and sporting events are sponsored by advertising. Today advertising is a huge business, with more than $300 billion spent globally.

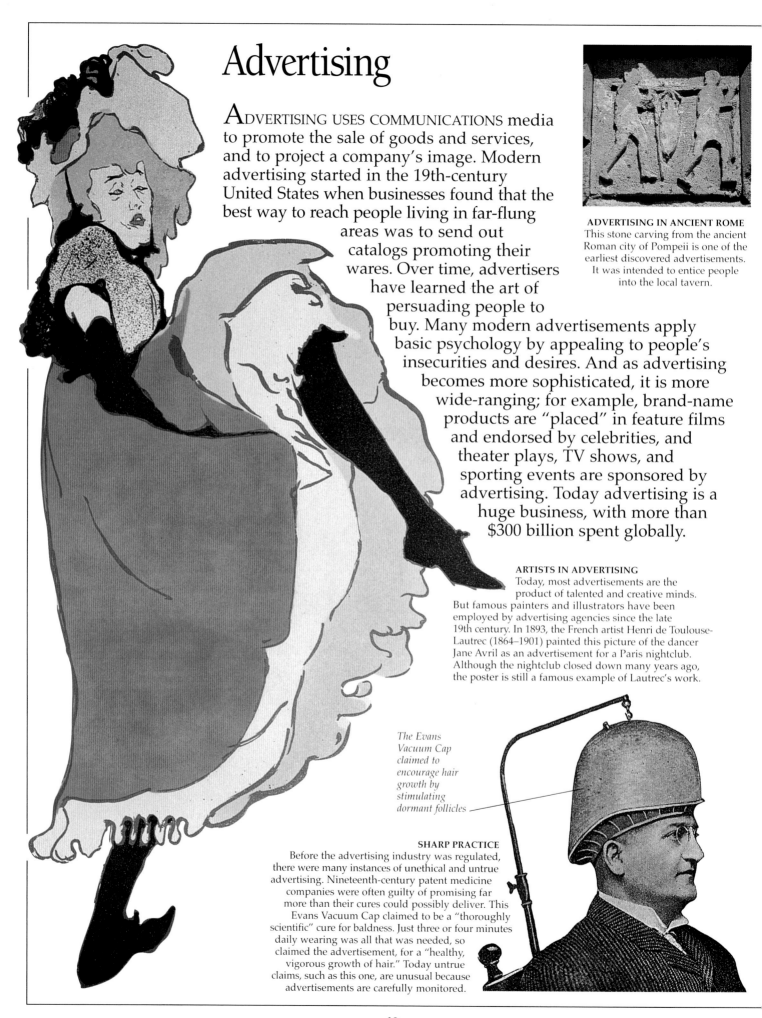

ADVERTISING IN ANCIENT ROME
This stone carving from the ancient Roman city of Pompeii is one of the earliest discovered advertisements. It was intended to entice people into the local tavern.

ARTISTS IN ADVERTISING
Today, most advertisements are the product of talented and creative minds. But famous painters and illustrators have been employed by advertising agencies since the late 19th century. In 1893, the French artist Henri de Toulouse-Lautrec (1864–1901) painted this picture of the dancer Jane Avril as an advertisement for a Paris nightclub. Although the nightclub closed down many years ago, the poster is still a famous example of Lautrec's work.

The Evans Vacuum Cap claimed to encourage hair growth by stimulating dormant follicles

SHARP PRACTICE
Before the advertising industry was regulated, there were many instances of unethical and untrue advertising. Nineteenth-century patent medicine companies were often guilty of promising far more than their cures could possibly deliver. This Evans Vacuum Cap claimed to be a "thoroughly scientific" cure for baldness. Just three or four minutes daily wearing was all that was needed, so claimed the advertisement, for a "healthy, vigorous growth of hair." Today untrue claims, such as this one, are unusual because advertisements are carefully monitored.

CAR THIEVES THROWN OUT OF "WORK"
BY THE DONFORD CAR LOCK
SEE IT AT DORLAND HALL
LOWER REGENT ST. W.1

FELTON'S
5,880 CARS STOLEN
IN THE METROPOLITAN POLICE AREA IN 1932
MAKE YOUR CAR THIEF-PROOF
DONFORD WAY
DEMONSTRATIONS AT DORLAND HALL
LOWER REGENT STREET W1
ADMISSION FREE

Broken glass symbolizes the tires' strength

Cigar smoking was a popular habit

The first Michelin man, in 1898

CHANGING LOGOS

With the arrival of brand-name goods in the 1880s, companies started to use distinctive graphics and lettering to make their products stand out. One result of this was the invention of a figure or image, called a logo, designed to represent the company or product. One of the most successful logos, to this day, is the tire-clad figure of the Michelin man, the symbol of Michelin tires. Invented in 1898, the Michelin man has undergone several alterations over the years.

1910s Michelin man

SANDWICH BOARD MEN

The simplest advertising is intended merely to inform the public of services or goods being offered. Print media, such as leaflets and local newspapers, are most often used for this type of promotion. And in the 1930s, sandwich board men were widely employed as walking advertisements.

CONSUMER BOOM

In the 1950s, high wages and full employment prompted a consumer boom in many western countries. Luxury goods, such as this washing machine, were being produced more cheaply than ever before. Much advertising for the new, easy-to-use goods suggested that owning them would bring glamour and increased social status.

1980s Michelin man is leaner, friendlier, non-smoking, and more muscular than fat

Wringer for drying clothes is attached

1980s Michelin man

Illustration depicts a glamorous, carefree woman

MILKY BAR KID

Television provides advertisers with the opportunity to use basic storytelling techniques, such as simple plots and recognizable characters, that hold people's attention while the advertising message is transmitted. The Milky Bar Kid, right, was created to sell a white chocolate bar in a series of such advertisements in the 1970s, and was so popular that the character was revived and updated for the 1990s.

Child actor playing the Milky Bar Kid

ADVERTISING EVERYWHERE

Visitors to the Shinjuku district of Tokyo, Japan, are dazzled by the array of neon signs. Advertising is difficult to avoid almost everywhere in the world, but without it much of the mass media would not exist. Commercial television and radio stations, along with most newspapers and magazines, could not survive without the revenue brought in by advertising.

Mass marketing

PEPSI-COLA STARTED LIFE in 1893 as "Brad's Drink" in honor of its inventor, the pharmacist Caleb Bradham. In 1898, the soft drink became known as Pepsi-Cola, later just Pepsi. The campaigns and slogans used to advertise the drink have changed regularly. A company, such as PepsiCo, changes the advertising of an established product both to reflect changes in society and to attract new consumers. In the budget-conscious 1930s, Pepsi was promoted as a value-for-money product. Twenty years later, the drink was portrayed as distinctly glamorous. During the 1980s, PepsiCo launched a campaign aimed at the growing youth market. In 1996, "Project Blue" — the title given to the change of Pepsi packaging from red to blue — was an attempt to widen the drink's appeal further. More than $300 million was spent on advertising the change.

GLAMOROUS PEPSI
Sometimes an established product requires a change of image because its consumers have changed their spending habits. In the 1950s, Pepsi's advertising was altered to appeal to a newly affluent public. Advertisements, such as the one above, depicted drinking Pepsi as a glamorous and sexy experience.

1950s Pepsi advertisement

THE BUSINESS OF ADVERTISING
In the 1920s, businesses started to employ advertising agencies to come up with new slogans and ideas for campaigns. Advertising became a profession. Agencies carried out research to find out what the public looks for in a particular product, and creative staffs used the results to promote the product in the most effective way possible.

Glass bottle was larger than those used by rival companies

CELEBRITY ENDORSEMENTS
Celebrities have endorsed or advertised products for decades. International products, such as Pepsi, prefer to use world-famous stars. In 1984, the pop star Michael Jackson was chosen to represent Pepsi's latest slogan: "The choice of a new generation."

PACKAGING DESIGN
Packaging design is an often overlooked area of advertising. Well-designed packaging can be produced efficiently, is popular with consumers, and reinforces the brand image. Pepsi was originally sold in glass bottles, but in 1948 it was produced in a can for the first time.

1940s Pepsi bottle

Steel can from the 1960s

Air France Concorde

PEPSI GOES SUPERSONIC

As part of "Project Blue," PepsiCo arranged for a Concorde, a supersonic aircraft that has a distinctly forward-looking image, to be painted with the new Pepsi graphics. It took 2,000 working hours and 79 gallons (300 liters) of paint to transform the aircraft. The Concorde displayed its new paintwork on an eight-day, ten-city tour of Europe and the Middle East.

Concorde displayed Pepsi's new graphics to thousands of people

PEPSI TOWER

While most advertising reaches us by the broadcast media, outdoor displays and signs promoting a company or brand-name are also used. Thousands of billboards and neon signs all over the world helped to launch Pepsi's new image in 1996, including this illuminated sign on the famous Blackpool Tower in the north of England.

Pepsi is sold in a local shop in Russia

NEW MARKETS

Global products rely on their worldwide image for sales, though they also tailor some advertising to particular countries. In Russia, the campaign to launch Pepsi's new blue design included promotional events, such as a free pop concert, as well as billboard and television advertising. With these events, PepsiCo set out to convince the Russian people that Pepsi is as essential as bread and milk.

1990s aluminum Pepsi can

1990s Diet Pepsi can

Low-calorie Pepsi was first introduced in 1964

CHINESE WHISPERS

Big companies expand by finding new markets. In 1983, PepsiCo became the first major foreign drinks manufacturer in China. By 2002, this country will be the largest soft drinks market. But selling in a new country can mean making changes to the way products are advertised, and sometimes this can lead to misunderstandings. In China, the slogan "Pepsi Comes Alive" was mistranslated to mean "Pepsi brings your ancestors back from the grave."

Persuasive propaganda

PROPAGANDA IS THE ORGANIZED circulation of information designed to influence people about certain things. It attempts to appeal directly to people's emotions or prejudices, and it may contain huge distortions of the truth. Propaganda can be spread by many different media, although posters, leaflets, radio, and the movies are among the most widely used. The first propaganda involved the spread of ancient religious and political views, but modern propaganda started with World War I. It was used to encourage a country's people to support the war effort, to damage the war effort in enemy countries, and to attempt to get neutral countries to take sides. Although mainly a wartime device, propaganda is used in peacetime by special interest or pressure groups.

PATRIOTIC PROPAGANDA
This famous 1915 poster of General Kitchener, by Alfred Leete, was designed to encourage British male civilians to enlist, or join up, with the armed forces fighting in World War I. The deliberate use of a heroic image with the finger pointing directly at the viewer, together with an appeal to pride in one's country (known as patriotism), created a powerful image.

"YOUR COUNTRY NEEDS YOU"

Chaplin as Adenoid Hynkel

CHAPLIN PLAYS HITLER
Much propaganda is aimed at belittling opponents or enemies, making them appear stupid and untrustworthy. This was the aim of the 1940 film *The Great Dictator*. Starring Charlie Chaplin as both a Jewish barber and a thinly disguised Adolf Hitler character called Adenoid Hynkel, it lampooned (made fun of) Hitler and the German Nazi Party's policies.

Communist Korean soldier trampling innocent people

¡ ESTAMOS VIGILANDOTE !

A warning to Nicaraguan people that they were constantly being watched

Anti-American Christmas card of the Vietnamese communists

Merry Christmas

WARTIME WORDS
Propaganda in wartime is frequently targeted at the enemy population, attempting to lower morale or encourage uprisings against the enemy government. Propaganda leaflets may be dropped by air into enemy territory or spread in secret operations with the help of rebel movements.

JUNTA DELEGADA DE DEFENSA DE MADRID
DELEGACION DE PROPAGANDA Y PRENSA

LA GARRA DEL INVASOR ITALIANO PRETENDE ESCLAVIZARNOS

THE FASCIST CLAW
This Republican poster from the Spanish Civil War of 1936–1939 portrays the opposing fascist forces as a terrible dark claw spreading across Spain. Much propaganda has been concerned with making enemies appear more evil and immoral than they may really be. This approach is intended to instill fear and encourage people to fight against the evil foe.

Sickle symbolizes the agricultural worker

The hammer is a symbol of the factory worker

The stainless-steel figures are young, strong, and attractive, portraying the communist ideal

Chairman Mao is depicted as the father of communism

LITTLE RED BOOKS
China's communist leader Mao Zedong wrote a book of propagandist sayings, called the *Little Red Book*, which became compulsory reading during the Cultural Revolution (1966). The foreword to the book demanded: "Study Chairman Mao's writings, and act according to his instructions."

HAPPY COMMUNISM
While much propaganda instructs, informs, or seeks to give negative messages about opposing viewpoints, some propaganda is intended to glorify the present situation with the promise of a much brighter future. The Soviet leader Joseph Stalin made considerable use of this form of propaganda with posters such as this one from 1946, portraying happy people thanking Stalin for his efforts.

THE GLORIOUS SOVIET FUTURE
One of the Soviet Union's strongest recurring images was the hammer and the sickle (a small handheld scythe), which was designed to represent a uniting of factory and farm workers, and town and country. This statue, called *Worker and Peasant Looking into the Glorious Communist Future*, was the symbol of the large government-controlled film studio, Mosfilm.

Perception and interpretation

PERCEPTION IS THE PROCESS whereby data received by our senses are converted by the brain into meaningful information. To do this, we need to interpret the meaning of the message. And if the message is to be communicated successfully, it has to be interpreted as its creator intended. Sometimes, mistakes occur because a message unintentionally carries more than one meaning. On other occasions, a message may deliberately contain more than one meaning. Artists, psychologists, and advertisers sometimes try to confuse our perception to make their work more powerful, to provide insights about the mind, or to challenge particular attitudes.

NAKED PERCEPTION
"The Emperor's New Clothes" is a tale that illustrates how our perception can be influenced by other people, especially those in authority. The emperor is convinced that he is wearing the finest, lightest clothes ever made when, in fact, he is naked. His advisers do not dare challenge him, so they accept his delusion and everyone else goes along with the majority opinion.

Illustration from "The Emperor's New Clothes"

INTERPRETING INKBLOTS
The Swiss psychologist Hermann Rorschach (1884–1922) devised a test in which people were asked to say what they thought ink-blots, as shown right, most resembled. He believed that each person's interpretation of an abstract image was an essential clue to his or her innermost thoughts.

TWO FACES AND A VASE
This simple drawing highlights the fact that visual perception is not always straightforward. There are two distinct images in the picture; one of a vase against a brown background, the other of two people's profiles against a white background. Our brains perceive both, and can switch rapidly between the two images.

A swan's neck can become an elephant's trunk

The elephant's ears are a reflection of the swan's wings

SWANS AND ELEPHANTS
Many artists have used techniques that deliberately play with our perceptions. These techniques show that visual sense can be tricked by an optical illusion, or by carefully constructed imagery. This painting, called *Swans Reflecting Elephants*, © Salvador Dalí/Foundation Gala-Salvador Dalí/Dacs 1999, was painted by the famous Spanish artist Salvador Dalí (1904–1989) in 1937. Dalí transformed the reflections in the water of the swans and the trees into images of elephants.

Company name is discreetly placed

Poster for Benetton clothing company

1990s British Army recruitment poster

ABSTRACT ADVERTISING
The simplest advertising aims simply to repeat a brand name, but some seems to do the opposite. The poster above shows three happy children from different parts of the world — conveying a positive, global image — but we have to look quite carefully to find out exactly what is being advertised. The result is that the viewer is unsure how to interpret the image, and may spend time puzzling over its meaning.

SUBVERTING EXPECTATIONS
Messages that subvert (challenge) expectations can be very effective. This poster, designed to encourage black men to join the British Army, is a copy of a World War I recruitment poster, with the original figure of General Kitchener replaced by a black officer. It is intended to subvert the often unconscious assumption that an army officer is white.

The meaning of the photograph is altered when the ball is visible

President Kennedy addresses the people of Berlin, Germany

The original picture

The cropped picture used by the press

JUMPING FOR PEACE OR PLAYING BALL?
The meaning of a photograph can be altered by the context in which it is seen, and sometimes by how much of the picture is shown. A photograph of a child playing with a ball, above, was cropped by a journalist to remove the ball (left). It was published in a number of newspapers to illustrate a story about an IRA (Irish Republican Army) cease-fire. The picture implied that the child was jumping for joy at the news of the cease-fire.

I AM A JELLY DOUGHNUT
In 1963, President Kennedy made a historic speech to the people of the German city of Berlin. Kennedy wanted to say that he was from Berlin in his heart, and used the German words *Ich bin ein Berliner* ("I am a Berliner"). These had another meaning for Germans because *Berliner* also means a jelly doughnut. Sometimes, words can be ambiguous (have a double meaning) and are open to misinterpretation.

Secret communication

THROUGHOUT HISTORY, groups and individuals have needed to communicate with one another secretly. Governments' secret services work undercover to investigate covert activities in their own and other countries. During wartime, military information becomes a vital weapon and spies and intelligence gatherers are kept busy trying to discover the enemy's next move. In war and peacetime, information needs to be communicated to colleagues without falling into the wrong hands. Sometimes, the best way to communicate secretly is to conceal the method of communication. In other cases, transmissions are coded so that they are unrecognizable to the enemy.

MESSENGER PIGEONS
Specially trained pigeons have been used to deliver secret messages since Julius Caesar (100–44 B.C.) used them during his campaigns in France. During World War II, the Allies used half a million pigeons to carry secret messages in tiny canisters attached to their legs.

Eyes, ears, and lips on dress

ELIZABETHAN INTRIGUES
This portrait of Queen Elizabeth I of England contains a symbol of the activities of her secret service — the eyes, ears, and lips that decorate her dress. During her long reign (1558–1603), Elizabeth came under threat from various opponents, who planned to overthrow her and take the throne. Thanks to the activities of her secret service, all the plots against her were discovered and Elizabeth remained queen until her death.

DECIPHERING A CIPHER
Cipher wheels are one way of making messages unintelligible to anyone except the intended receiver. Letters or numbers are replaced with other letters or numbers by following the settings on the wheel. To decode the message, the receiver must know which setting of the cipher wheel has been used.

French biscuit tin

HIDDEN RADIO
This MCR 1 radio receiver, built during World War II, was used by members of the French resistance. It was fitted into a common biscuit tin (above) to disguise it from German forces during house searches. When the coast was clear, the components were quickly put together and tuned to British broadcasts. Many regular British radio programs — from dramatizations to weather forecasts — contained coded messages intended for resistance agents.

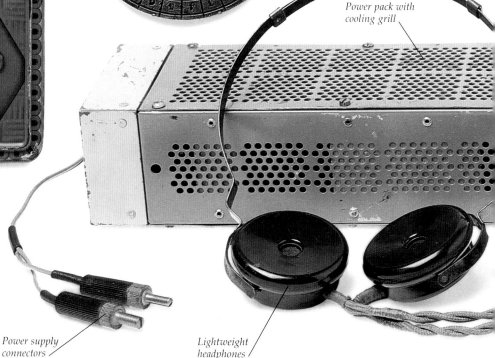

Power pack with cooling grill

Power supply connectors

Lightweight headphones

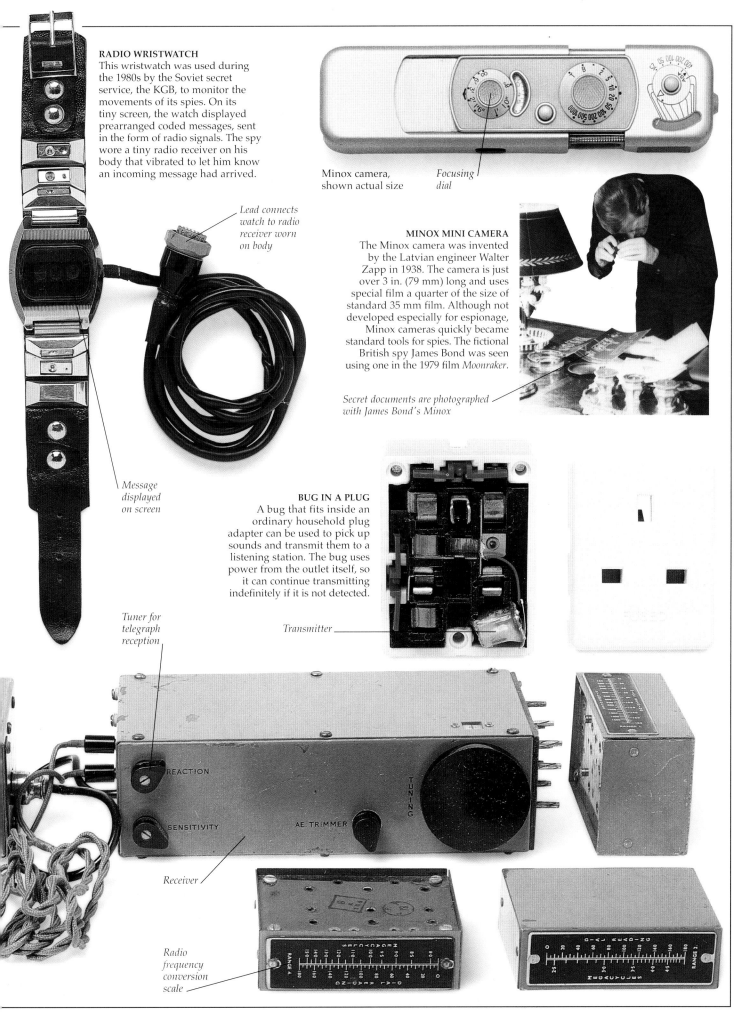

RADIO WRISTWATCH
This wristwatch was used during the 1980s by the Soviet secret service, the KGB, to monitor the movements of its spies. On its tiny screen, the watch displayed prearranged coded messages, sent in the form of radio signals. The spy wore a tiny radio receiver on his body that vibrated to let him know an incoming message had arrived.

Lead connects watch to radio receiver worn on body

Message displayed on screen

Minox camera, shown actual size

Focusing dial

MINOX MINI CAMERA
The Minox camera was invented by the Latvian engineer Walter Zapp in 1938. The camera is just over 3 in. (79 mm) long and uses special film a quarter of the size of standard 35 mm film. Although not developed especially for espionage, Minox cameras quickly became standard tools for spies. The fictional British spy James Bond was seen using one in the 1979 film *Moonraker*.

Secret documents are photographed with James Bond's Minox

BUG IN A PLUG
A bug that fits inside an ordinary household plug adapter can be used to pick up sounds and transmit them to a listening station. The bug uses power from the outlet itself, so it can continue transmitting indefinitely if it is not detected.

Transmitter

Tuner for telegraph reception

REACTION

SENSITIVITY

AE. TRIMMER

TUNING

Receiver

Radio frequency conversion scale

Emergency communication

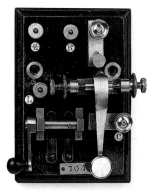

A WARNING MESSAGE may help to prevent an accident. And if a disaster arises, quick and accurate communication can help save lives. The stricken victims need to let others know of their predicament so that assistance can be organized. Rescuers need to communicate with each other and with the victims, often in hazardous conditions and some distance away from civilization. Before the arrival of advanced communication devices, such as lightweight radios and mobile phones, many ingenious methods, from flares to flags, were used to warn people of approaching danger or to announce distress.

DOTS AND DASHES
Morse code uses a series of dots and dashes to represent the alphabet; they are tapped in with a key, such as the one above. Morse is transmitted either with a flashing light or via a telegraph system, and was used for emergency communication until February 1999. The first SOS signal (three dots, then three dashes, then three more dots) was sent by the *Titanic* on April 15, 1912, the night it sank.

The light is visible from 16 miles (25 kilometers) away

WARNING LIGHTS
Lighthouses and lightships have been used for centuries to warn sailors of rocks or shallow seas. They are still used as warnings for marine craft, but today most are uncrewed, like this large automatic navigational buoy known as a Lanby. The Lanby measures 40 feet (12 meters) across and carries a radar beacon and foghorn as well as its powerful light.

The buoy can be moored in water up to 300 feet (90 meters) deep

Tony Bullimore is lifted to safety

EMERGENCY RESCUE
In January 1997, lone yachtsman Tony Bullimore's life was placed in danger when his yacht capsized in the hostile Pacific Ocean. Bullimore took shelter in a small air pocket beneath the upturned yacht and banged on the side of the hull to attract attention. The sound was picked up by a sonar buoy. After 89 hours, Bullimore was rescued and went on to make a full recovery.

Filter prevents inhalation of noxious fumes

TELEPHONE GAS MASK
Communication channels must be kept open whenever there is an emergency or disaster. During wartime, special equipment is often called for. This World War II headgear, for example, combined a gas mask with a telephone operator's headset, so that telephone calls, especially vital ones, could still be made, even in the event of a major release of harmful gas.

This semaphore
signaler is spelling
out the word "H-E-L-P"

*Flags are always
held with the
arms extended
so that they can
be seen clearly*

H   E   L   P

FLAG SIGNALS
A system of communicating
with flags, known as
semaphore, was invented and
developed in the 18th century
by a French schoolboy, Claude
Chappé. Two flags are held in
different positions to represent
the letters of the alphabet.
Semaphore was later adopted
for ship-to-shore and some
land communications.

FLAGGING A PROBLEM
Flags have been used for many
centuries to communicate basic
messages from hilltop to hilltop and
between ships at sea. A standardized
system for maritime flags was
introduced in the 19th century.
The flags represent both letters
and numbers and have particular
meanings. For example, the flag
above means: "You are steering
toward the center of a typhoon."

*Message-
receiving
headphones*

*Handheld flares
burn with an
orange, red,
or white light*

SCHERMULY

FROG HORN

FLARES AND FOGHORNS
Flares and foghorns are used to
communicate distress and indicate
location for a search or rescue party.
Foghorns use compressed air from
a cylinder to make an ear-piercing
noise. Flares are are either handheld
or launched into the air and burn
brightly for up to several minutes.

*The operator
speaks into this
mouthpiece*

Telephone operator's
gas mask, made in 1938

Toxic/
poisonous

Radioactive

WARNING SIGNS
Simple pictures or symbols are used all over
the world to convey easily recognizable
warnings. They have been devised to alert
people to the dangers of harmful materials
or equipment. These symbols, such as those
pictured right, are often seen on freight
carriers or in factories and laboratories.

The computer revolution

IN ITS SHORT LIFE of less than half a century, the computer has revolutionized the way we communicate. Computer technology has given some people — those with a physical or mental disability, for instance — the means to communicate clearly for the first time. Computers have also become a valuable teaching aid in schools. In the workplace, many businesses rely on computers for communication and for performing mundane tasks, and some use computer-controlled robots. This means that much unskilled work is no longer available for humans, resulting in unemployment. And, of course, computing has generated new forms of media and ways of communicating, such as the Internet and virtual reality.

A PIONEER COMPUTER
ENIAC was a pioneering computing machine built in the United States in the 1940s. Weighing an incredible 30 tons, ENIAC filled a room 40 ft (13 m) x 20 ft (6.5 m). All early computers were capable of performing only single tasks, and ENIAC was programmed to calculate the height, force, and range of new bombs, rockets, and missiles under development.

COMPACT COMPUTER
As computer technology has developed, smaller and smaller machines contain the computing power that would have filled a large room 20 years ago. This 1998 laptop computer has all the power of bulky desktop machines. A built-in modem allows the user to communicate with other computers on the Internet.

Robot arm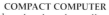

Touchpad for moving cursor around screen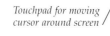

High-resolution color screen

MACHINE TO MACHINE
Much factory work is now performed by computer-controlled robots. This Ford Mondeo car assembly line in Belgium features a number of robots linked to a computer controller, which sends data to the robots and receives feedback data in return. Two-way communication enables the robots to carry out a whole series of tasks.

COMPUTER ART
Computers are often used to do much of the monotonous work required in creating other forms of media. This computer-controlled robotic artist goes one stage further. A computer program, called AARON, generates its own original artwork, which is then painted by the robot arm. The arm can change brushes and mix paints as required.

Piece of metal type

PUBLISHING MADE EASY

Computers and desktop publishing (DTP) software have made publishing a much simpler business. Now, typesetting is performed automatically, and books are created entirely on computers. They can be sent directly to the printers on a phone line. Some companies also publish CD-ROMs, which store text and images in digital form and can be only "read" with a computer.

TYPESETTING

Before computers, books and newspapers were typeset laboriously by hand. Every letter, punctuation mark, and space had its own piece of metal type. Each line of type was arranged on a special tray called a galley, and great care had to be taken not to make mistakes. Typesetting was a difficult task and could be performed only by specially trained workers.

Professor Hawking selects appropriate words from a display on the screen

MAKING A VOICE

The renowned British physicist Stephen Hawking (1942–□) suffers from a debilitating disease and is unable to talk. He relies on a voice synthesizer connected to a computer. The synthesizer "speaks" the words Professor Hawking enters on the screen. The entire system is built into his wheelchair, enabling him to make speeches and give lectures.

LEARNING TOOL

Computer-assisted learning is becoming an increasingly important supplement to traditional teaching media. Educational software encourages pupils to learn, practice, and repeat skills in a range of subjects. The computer can assist pupils and immediately mark their work.

Virtual reality

Virtual reality headset

VIRTUAL REALITY (VR) is a simulation of a real or invented environment created with advanced computer technology. VR worlds can be viewed on 180° video screens, or on special headsets containing small display screens. Data gloves or special suits that provide a simulated sense of touch might also be worn. VR is so realistic that it can give users the impression that they are actually inside the simulated environment. VR was first developed in the 1960s to help train pilots. Although still in its infancy, VR has many uses. It is helping to train surgeons and astronauts, and to design safer cars. VR is also being used to re-create the past; buildings and even cities that disappeared long ago are being reconstructed by VR.

VIRTUAL ENTERTAINMENT
VR has been used to make computer games a three-dimensional experience. The games are displayed either on a computer screen or on a headset, as above. The scene changes as the player moves his or her head and interacts with the game with a joystick or some other controller.

1 DISCOVERY OF A FRESCO
This fresco of a city was painted on a wall in the Domus Aurea, the palace of the Roman emperor Nero in the 1st century A.D. It was discovered in 1998 and, at 9 x 12 ft (2.7 x 3.6 m), is the largest known Roman fresco of a city. A high-resolution scan (digital image) of the fresco enabled historians to examine it in great detail.

Towered stone wall encircles the city

City wall reconstructed

2 FRESCO CITY MODEL
Historians believed that the city shown in the fresco was an imperial Roman settlement. Using the scan of the fresco, virtual reality artists were able to build a simulation of the city, providing VR users with a unique opportunity to explore an ancient settlement.

Bright green indicates severe damage

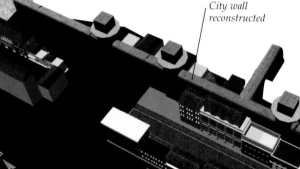

VR CRASH TESTING
Car manufacturers are using VR to find out exactly what happens to the structure and components of a car when it crashes. This VR simulation of a crash uses different colors to represent varying levels of stress in the car's body. Engineers can replay the crash over and over again, pause it at any stage, zoom in to look closer, and even strip away parts of the car's body to look at the damage underneath.

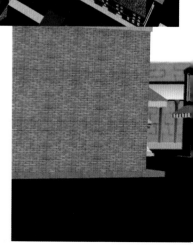

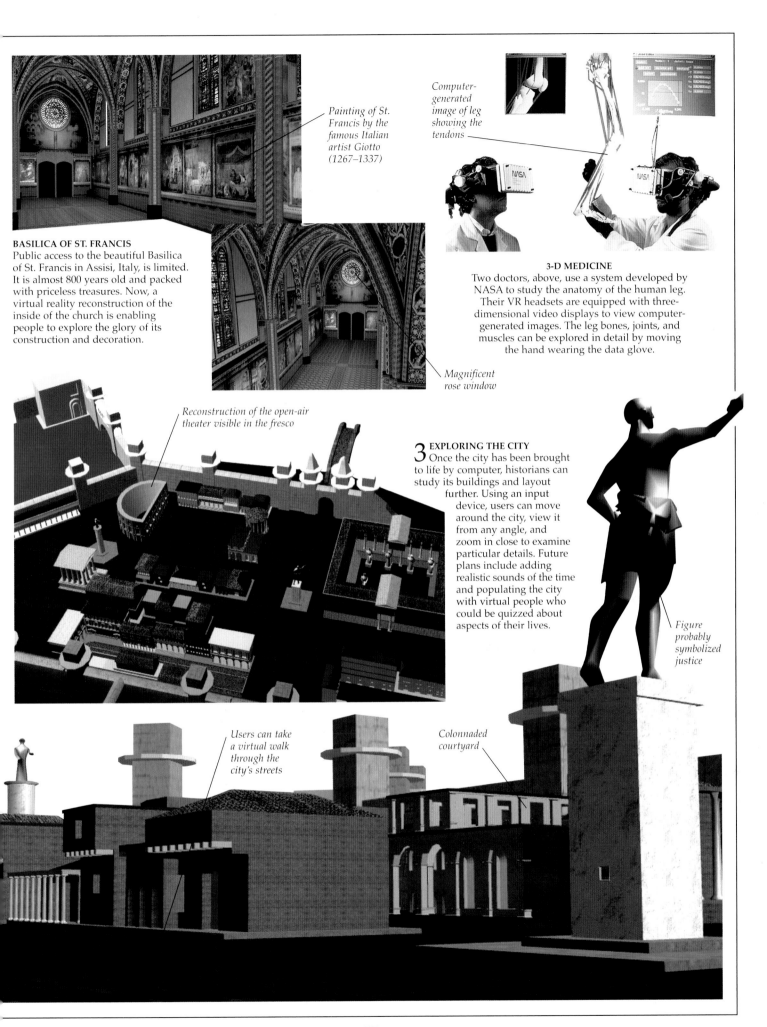

Painting of St. Francis by the famous Italian artist Giotto (1267–1337)

Computer-generated image of leg showing the tendons

BASILICA OF ST. FRANCIS
Public access to the beautiful Basilica of St. Francis in Assisi, Italy, is limited. It is almost 800 years old and packed with priceless treasures. Now, a virtual reality reconstruction of the inside of the church is enabling people to explore the glory of its construction and decoration.

3-D MEDICINE
Two doctors, above, use a system developed by NASA to study the anatomy of the human leg. Their VR headsets are equipped with three-dimensional video displays to view computer-generated images. The leg bones, joints, and muscles can be explored in detail by moving the hand wearing the data glove.

Magnificent rose window

Reconstruction of the open-air theater visible in the fresco

3 EXPLORING THE CITY
Once the city has been brought to life by computer, historians can study its buildings and layout further. Using an input device, users can move around the city, view it from any angle, and zoom in close to examine particular details. Future plans include adding realistic sounds of the time and populating the city with virtual people who could be quizzed about aspects of their lives.

Figure probably symbolized justice

Users can take a virtual walk through the city's streets

Colonnaded courtyard

The Internet

THE FASTEST-GROWING MEDIUM today is the Internet: a worldwide network of millions of computers. The Internet started life in 1969 as a top-secret military project, developed in the United States. The project's aim was to create a secure computer network that could survive damage to part of its systems. In the 1980s, the Internet was established as an effective way for academics to share knowledge, and by the early 1990s, the general public was using it for education, entertainment, and business. A few years later, the number of people using the Internet was growing by about one million each month.

THE WORLD IN YOUR HOME
From the comfort of home, computer owners can tap into the world's biggest information bank, the World Wide Web. Thousands of web sites (networks of "pages") relating to almost any topic can be accessed. Text, pictures, and even video and sound can be saved onto the user's own computer. Gathering information has never been so easy.

Diagram shows the layout of Paris's Louvre gallery

The Mona Lisa known as La Gioconda, 1503-1506, Leonardo da Vinci
The Italian School The Renaissance

A selection of paintings from the Louvre gallery

ART FOR EVERYONE
Many museums, libraries, and art galleries have put part or all of their collections on the Internet. Computer users anywhere in the world can view these collections on their screens by simply visiting the appropriate web site. Thousands of high-quality images and important background information are available to anyone with access to the Internet.

An avatar, controlled by the user

WORLDWIDE FRIENDS
Web sites called chat rooms allow users to type messages to each other with no delay between sending and receiving, a facility called "real time." Some chat rooms, such as *Worldsaway*, right, are virtual worlds, created with computer graphics, where each user controls a figure called an avatar. Avatars have a range of movements and expressions to make communication lifelike.

SHOPPING ON THE INTERNET
For little cost, individuals and small businesses, as well as big companies, can set up their own web sites and advertise their wares to a potential audience of millions. It is possible to buy anything from a rare book to a package of cereal on the Internet. Goods are paid for by credit card and delivered to the buyer's home.

:-)	Happy	:-))	Very happy
:-)	Winking	:-*	Kiss
:-(	Sad	:'-(	Crying
:-|	Hmmph!	:-||	Angry
:-†	Cross	:-X	Not speaking
:-&	Tongue-tied	:-/	Undecided
:-@	Screaming	:-V	Shouting
:-O	Shocked	|-O	Yawning

LANGUAGE OF THE INTERNET
Typing can be a slow way of communicating for some people, so users have developed shortcuts to speed up the process. Certain combinations of keyboard symbols, known as emoticons (emotional icons), are used to convey a mood or emotion quickly in a chat room or electronic mail.

INTERNET CAFÉ
Millions of people now have Internet access at school, at work, or at home. Those without direct access can visit a cyber café, where they can eat, drink, and for a small fee, hire a computer. Customers can log on to the Internet, gather information, and send and receive E-mail. E-mail is typed in at the keyboard and sent by telephone line, usually reaching its destination within minutes. Cheaper, more convenient, and much faster than conventional mail, E-mail has become a vital business tool and an easy way of keeping in touch with friends and family.

INTERNET ON THE MOVE
Portable Internet machines could have the same revolutionary effect on communication that personal stereos had on how we listen to music. People at work, like this engineer, could have access to huge amounts of reference material as well as instant visual and audio communication with experts on the other side of the world.

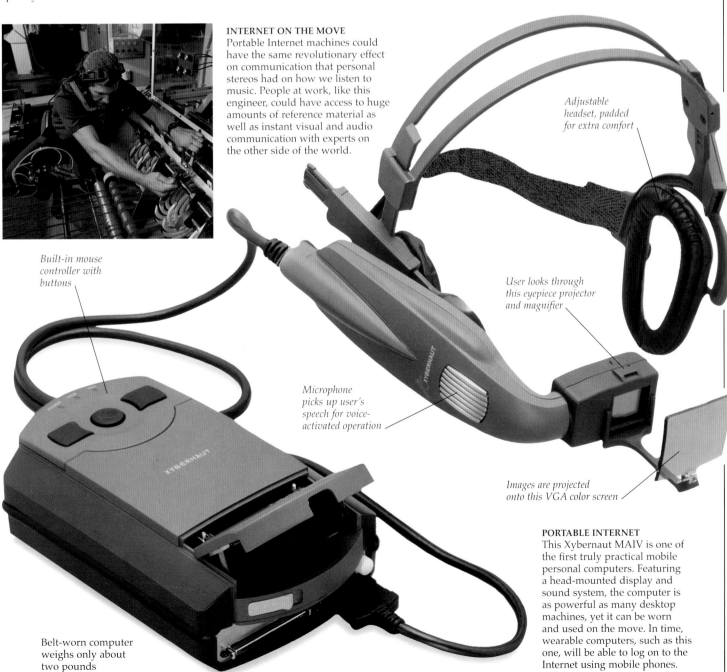

Adjustable headset, padded for extra comfort

Built-in mouse controller with buttons

User looks through this eyepiece projector and magnifier

Microphone picks up user's speech for voice-activated operation

Images are projected onto this VGA color screen

Belt-worn computer weighs only about two pounds

PORTABLE INTERNET
This Xybernaut MAIV is one of the first truly practical mobile personal computers. Featuring a head-mounted display and sound system, the computer is as powerful as many desktop machines, yet it can be worn and used on the move. In time, wearable computers, such as this one, will be able to log on to the Internet using mobile phones.

Future technology

THE STORY OF COMMUNICATION is far from over. New media, such as virtual reality and the Internet, are still evolving. The mass of information available to people is constantly increasing, and new ways of exploring it will be developed. Scientists are currently considering the possibility of implanting microprocessors in people's bodies. These could transmit information, such as personal identity and financial details, to a computer anywhere in the world, making identity and credit cards unnecessary. It may even become possible to transmit thoughts and feelings to another person in this way.

Implant is 1 in (23 mm) long

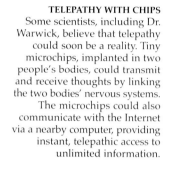

TELEPATHY WITH CHIPS
Some scientists, including Dr. Warwick, believe that telepathy could soon be a reality. Tiny microchips, implanted in two people's bodies, could transmit and receive thoughts by linking the two bodies' nervous systems. The microchips could also communicate with the Internet via a nearby computer, providing instant, telepathic access to unlimited information.

64 bit micro-processor

Circuit board

Electro-magnetic coil provides power

SCIENTIST BECOMES CYBORG
In August 1998, Dr. Kevin Warwick, professor of cybernetics at Britain's Reading University, became the subject of a revolutionary experiment. He had a microprocessor, capable of communicating with sensors and machines, implanted in his arm. It consists of a microchip, a tiny circuit board, and an electromagnet, and is housed in a sterilized glass container.

1 THE OPERATION
The implant was sewn under the skin of Dr. Warwick's forearm by a surgeon. Doctors were concerned that Dr. Warwick's immune system might reject the implant, or that the glass container could break inside his body. Luckily, neither of these things happened, and the implant remained in Dr. Warwick's arm for one week — the duration of the experiment.

2 SENSOR IN OPERATION
The circuitry inside the implant sends out signals, which are recognized by special sensors fitted in the university building. As Dr. Warwick walks toward his laboratory door, the signal from his implant is picked up by a sensor that automatically unlocks and opens the door. In the future, implants could replace door and car keys.

Dr. Warwick's web site is displayed

3 "GOOD MORNING, DR. WARWICK"
When Dr. Warwick sits down at his desk, the implant transmits a signal that switches on his computer. The computer greets Dr. Warwick with a voice message, downloads his own web site, and automatically displays his incoming E-mail.

Other worlds

Contacting alien life-forms is the greatest communication challenge. Even the nearest stars are a million times further away than our sun. So far, messages have been carried aboard space probes, and radio signals have been beamed into deep space. Meanwhile, humans continue to listen for incoming signals.

M13 STAR CLUSTER
Arecibo's message is traveling toward a dense cluster of stars called M13. It could take 25,000 years to reach its destination. If there are any life-forms within M13, they will need to be highly advanced in order to decode and understand the message.

MESSAGE IN SPACE
In 1974, a radio signal was sent out into deep space by the Arecibo radio telescope in Puerto Rico. It contains a series of pulses that can be arranged to form simple pictograms, which depict various aspects of humankind.

Double helix — the structure of DNA

The human figure

THE SOUNDS OF EARTH
The deep-space *Voyager* probe carries an LP record encoded with sounds and pictures that aim to sum up life on Earth. However, it will be 40,000 years before *Voyager* reaches any nearby stars.

LOOKING FOR LIFE
The Goldstone Tracking Station in California is part of the Search for Extraterrestial Intelligence (SETI) program. A powerful radio antenna fitted to a 230-ft- (70-m-) wide dish is seeking out signals from outer space by making a scan of the entire sky. It will take many years to complete the scan.

The earth, third planet from the sun

The sun

Radio signal message

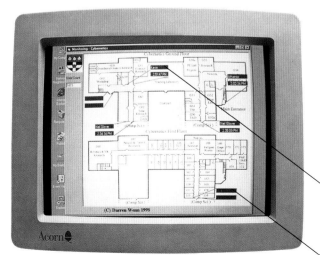

South American magazine

Dr. Warwick is in the teaching laboratory

Blue rectangle indicates the presence of a sensor

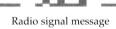

4 TRACKING DR. WARWICK
As Dr. Warwick moves around the university building, the implant sends out a signal indicating his current position. His secretary can find out where he is and in what direction he is headed by looking at this tracking monitor. Some other members of staff carry "smart cards" (equivalents of Dr. Warwick's microprocessor that are carried in a wallet), and they are also indicated on the monitor.

Indian magazine

5 WORLDWIDE ATTENTION
As a result of this experiment, Dr. Warwick has become a media celebrity. He has been featured in a wide range of publications and on television all over the world. Above are just some of the magazines that have highlighted his story; they are from France, Brazil, Germany, and India.

59

Index

Acknowledgments

Dorling Kindersley would like to thank:

Hayley Conway of the British Library, Neil Johannessen of Telecom Technology Showcase, Tom Fuke and Karen Reed of SiliconGraphics Computer Systems, Steve Newman of IBM, Professor Kevin Warwick of the Department of Cybernetics, University of Reading (pp. 58–59).
Editorial assistance: Fran Baines, Fergus Day, Fran Jones, Scarlett O'Hara, Helena Spiteri.
Design assistance: Polly Appleton, Venice Shone.
Research: Robert Graham.
Additional photography: Geoff Brightling, Tina Chambers, John Chase, Andy Crawford, Geoff Dann, Philip Dowell, Chris Dyer, Christi Graham and Nick Nicholls, Peter Hayman, Alan Hills, Lawrence Pardes, James Stevenson (NMM), Clive Streeter, Matthew Ward.
Illustrators: David Ashby, Joanne Connor, David Harris, John Woodcock.
Index: Chris Bernstein.
The publisher would like to thank the following for their kind permission to reproduce the following photographs:

(a=above, b=below, c=center, l=left, r=right, t=top)
Advertising Archives: 41 cl; AKG, London: 19t, 23 cr, 40 l, 45 cr, 47 br; Erich Lessing 16 bl, 18 b; Allsport: Ben Radford 37 bc; Apple Computer, Inc.: 6 br; 52 cr; Archivo Iconografico: The Auckland Collection: 44 bl; Bath Postal Museum: 22 bl; 22-23; BayGen Power Group: 33 br; BMG Interactive: Bridgeman Art Library, London: Emile Vernet, The Arab Tale Teller, 1833, The Wallace Collection, London 12 br, Atlas by Diogo Homem, map of South America, Add. 5415A f. 23v - 24, British Library 21 tl, Salvador Dalí, Swans Reflecting Elephants, ex-Edward James Foundation, Sussex, UK, Salvador Dalí/Foundation Gala-Salvador Dalí/Dacs 1999: 46 b; The British Library: 24 l, tc, 24-25 c, 25 br, cr, 4 br; 7; British Telecommunications plc: 4 tl; 5 tl, tr, c, 6 tr, ctr, cr, br; 28–29 all except br, 30 br, cl, tl, 31 tr, 50-51cc; CCS: 49cr; The image is reproduced with kind permission from the Coca-Cola company: 9r; Compuserve Information Services: 56 cl, c r; Corbis: 8 br, Gianni Dagli Orti 8 tl, 19 b, Bettmann/UPI 13 tr, 15 tc, 22 cl, cm, 32 cl, bl, 33 tl, 34 b, 36bl, 48 tl, 52 cl, Stephanie Maze 13 cl,

Richard Fukuhara 14 cr, Nathan Benn 15 cr, Hulton Getty 18 cr, 26t, 41 tl, Araldo de Luca 20 tl, David Holmes 21 br, David H. Wells 33 cr, 43 br, Michael Yamashita 35 cl, Underwood & Underwood 36 br, Mark Gibson 39 cl, Owen Franken 39 bc, Robert Maas 42 bl, Andrew Bell 43 cl, Wolfgang Kaehler 43 cr, Reg Ergenbright 45 tr, Dave Bartruff 45 b, Bob Rowan/Progressive Image 53 c, Jim Sugar Photography 53 br, Kevin Fleming 57 tr, NASA 59 tl, Roger Ressmeyer 59 c; Decorative Arts Association: 9t; ET Archive: 44 t; Mary Evans' Picture Library: 12 bl, 13 tl, 20 bl, 46 t; John Frost Newspapers: 26 br, 27 tl, bl, 33 tc, 38 cr, Solo Syndication 39 tl; FSN: 56 br; Galaxy Picture Lbrary: Palomar Sky Survey 59 tc; Glasgow Museum: Simon Alderson 36 t; Ronald Grant Archive: 34 c, 35 cr, 44 cl; Robert Harding Picture Library/Paul van Riel: 52 bc; Hulton Getty: 53 tl; IBM: 4 bl, 57 cl, b; Imperial War Museum: 48–49 b; David King Collection: 26 cl, bl; Kobal Collection: 9 cl, 49 ct; Museum of London: 17; H.K. Melton: 49 tr; Michelin Tyre Plc: 41 tc, tr, cr; Moviestore Collection: 35 tr, cl, bl, br; NASA: 37 tc; Nestlé: 41 bl; Robert Opie Collection: 23 cl; 42 t, bc, br; Panos Pictures:

Caroline Penn 13 cr, Eric Miller 10 bl; Pepsi: 43 tl; Punch: 18 cl; Pictor International: 15 tl; Popperfoto: 36 bc; Rex Features: 14 tl, Des Johnson 33 tr, Southwest News Services 38 tl, cl, bl, 38-39, 40 tr, Crispin Rodwell 47 cl, bl, Sipa 50 c; by courtesy of the Marquess of Salisbury/The Fotomas Index: 48 tr; Science Photo Library: Alfred Pasieka 30 bl, Mike Agiolo 30-31, Simon Fraser 31 tl, David Ducros 39 c, Hank Morgan 52 br, Gable, Jerrican 56 t; SiliconGraphics: 54 b, ACS Studio 54 cl, c, cr, 54-5 b, 55c, Infobyte 55 tl; Solo Syndication: 39 br; Southwest News Services: 39 tr; Frank Spooner Pictures/Gamma: Hartung/Liaison 25 tr, 47 tr; Tony Stone Images: Peter Correz 14 cl, Chad Ehlers 41 br, Bruce Ayres 42cl; © Times Newspapers Limited, 11th May 1958, 31st March 1999: 27 cl, 27 tr; United Colors of Benetton: 47 tl.

Jacket:
BayGen Power Group front ctl; AKG London back ctr; Historical Newspaper Service back bc; Apple Macintosh back br; Ronald Grant Archive inside front tl; SiliconGraphics, Reading, inside front br.